Managing Anger

A Handbook of Proven Techniques

Mitchell H. Messer, M.A.

Roman Coronado-Bogdaniak, M.D., M.H.S.

Linda J. Dillon, B.A., R.Hy.

C.O.P.E. PUBLICATIONS
THE ANGER CLINIC
111 N. Wabash, Suite 1702
Chicago, Illinois 60602
312-263-0035

To Len Kreusler,
all the best
Mitchell Messer
2/10/98

Illustrations © Robert Johnson.   Photo by Jerry Sharff.

ISBN 1-881416-00-3

Printed and bound in the United States of America.

First Edition.   First Printing October, 1992.

93 94 95 10 9 8 7 6 5 4 3 2 1

C.O.P.E. Publications are available at quantity discounts with bulk purchase for educational, business or sales promotional use. Inquiries should be addressed to Premium Marketing Division, C.O.P.E. Publications, a subsidiary of Community Outreach, Prevention and Education, Inc., 8746 Park Lane, Niles, IL 60714, (708) 662-6233.

Library of Congress Cataloging-in-Publication Data

Messer, Mitchell
        Managing anger: a handbook of proven techniques/ Mitchell H. Messer, Roman Coronado-Bogdaniak, Linda J. Dillon.
        p. cm. -- (the emotional first aid series for you and your loved ones)
Includes bibliographical references and index
ISBN 1-881416-00-3 (paper)
        1. Anger. 2. Interpersonal conflict. I. Coronado-Bogdaniak, Roman, 1954-   II. Dillon, Linda J., 1947-   III. Title. IV. Series.
BF575.A5M488 1992   92-18895
152.4'7--dc20   CIP

DEDICATION

This book is dedicated to the
memory of Dr. Rudolph Dreikurs.
He was our teacher.
He is still our teacher.

ACKNOWLEDGMENTS

We wish to acknowledge the patience and skill of all the unsung people behind the scenes, without whose efforts this book would have remained a glimmer in its authors' eyes. Our thanks go to Ann Aler, Ann Rymsza, Rebecca Cady Patton, Jan Jones, Lorraine Dillon, the staff at A-OK Business Service and a special thanks to Kathleen Welton of AKA Associates. Thanks also to Paul J. Dillon, Sr., Maria Coronado-Bogdaniak and Joyce Messer who lent moral support and emotional first aid to our endeavors when we needed it, which was most of the time.

IN MEMORIAM

Roman Coronado-Bagdoniak, M.D.
1954-1993

ABOUT THE AUTHORS

Mitchell H. Messer, M.A.

Mitch Messer received his Master's Degree in Clinical Psychology from Roosevelt University. He took his advanced work in counseling psychology at the Alfred Adler Institute of Chicago. He has served with the Suicide Prevention Service of the State of Illinois Department of Mental Health and is a marriage and family counselor in private practice. Mr. Messer has been a management consultant with the American Telephone and Telegraph Co. and Illinois Bell Telephone. He is a consultant with the Chicago Board of Education, the Cook County Educational Service Region. As the Director of the Anger Clinic, he has been a frequent guest on television and radio, both locally and nationally, including the Phil Donahue Show, Two on Two, New Day Chicago and the Geraldo Rivera Show.

Roman Coronado-Bogdaniak, M.D., M.H.S., N.C.A.C. II

Dr. Roman has been the Executive Director of Community Outreach, Prevention and Education, Inc. since 1984 and is the Program Director of the C.O.P.E. Training Institute. He has been a faculty member and department chair at numerous universities, colleges and hospital-based programs. Dr. Roman created the first bilingual, bicultural addictions counselor training programs in the world and is a renowned international presenter, popular media figure and the author of numerous professional publications. He is considered to be one of the foremost experts in the field on cultural aspects and special population issues.

Linda J. Dillon, B.A., R.Hy.

Linda Dillon studied at Wisconsin University, Western Illinois University and received her degree in psychology at Governor's State University. She is presently doing advanced work at The Alfred Adler Institute in Chicago. Linda is a member of the American Association of Counseling and Development, The North American Society of Adlerian Psychology as well as a certified hypnotherapist registered with the Hypnodyne Foundation. As Assistant Director of The Anger Clinic, Linda recently produced and hosted a very successful 13-week educational television series called The Anger Hotline.

iv

TABLE OF CONTENTS

INTRODUCTION

By this time, you may have read many books on dysfunctional families, co-dependency, communication, shame, violence, abuse, guilt, addiction and grief. There are plenty of books on these subjects, but very few on the subject of anger. These other topics are important, but anger is the specific emotion that can destroy your marriage, your relationship with your loved ones or your job -- in fact, it is the emotion that can blow up this planet. So why are we so strangely reluctant to take this powerful emotion as seriously as it needs to be taken? Anger is like a crazy relative in the attic that everyone knows is there but no one talks about.

That is the problem. Anger is an emotion that causes terrible damage every day, but no one wants to talk about it because it isn't nice. If we do talk about it, we are told to hit a pillow with a bat, walk around the block or think happy thoughts. Even professional counselors are shy about confronting this scary emotion. Understandably, most counselors feel inadequately prepared to cope with anger problems because there is no course in Angerology 101 in our counselor preparation institutions.

You may have been told that you are "aggressive," "bitchy" or "hostile." There is no cure for being hostile, but there are many ways to relieve your legitimate, valid anger. Despite what you have been hearing all your life, you are not a bad person if you get angry. Nice people like you get angry all the time, but they have learned to manage it between the extremes of too much (erupting like a volcano) and too little (smiling through your tears).

In this book, you will learn how you can manage your anger. You will learn that you can stop feeling frustrated, depressed or anxious very quickly. You will learn that you have choices that you didn't know you had. When you exercise your power of choice, these joy-killing hangovers from the past will finally begin to go away. You will be able to stop existing and start living.

1

Do you wonder why you are walking around talking to yourself feeling confused, dissatisfied, discouraged or "out of it" as they say these days? It is because life gives us an anger problem every twelve minutes, which we are inadequately prepared to solve. Sometimes these problems escalate until we can't stand it. These problems are painful to us. Our pain is compounded by our anger at ourselves for not being able to solve them. It is not our fault that we never learned anger management techniques before this. This book is your resource for filling this void in your education and relieving your pain.

Managing Anger

In our twenty years of experience at the Anger Clinic in Chicago, we have seen the terrible things that mismanaged anger can do to a marriage, a career and a life. We have also seen how quickly this damage can be repaired, even reversed, when people are given tools that they did not even know existed. Marriages on the brink of disaster have been turned around when destructive anger practices were replaced by interventions that made things better instead of worse. Employees facing the choice of quitting or being fired have learned how to cope successfully with their boss's childish temper tantrums to the benefit of themselves, the boss and everyone in the division.

Even insoluble anger problems from forty years ago can be relieved. By putting them in a new perspective so that they do not have to be solved, they can be drained out of our system in the right way so that we can get on with our lives with more energy and joy than we had before.

One of our anger management tools, for instance, is the power of choice. People keep making the same mistakes because no one ever told them what their options were. They come in feeling discouraged and unable to cope because they only have one anger choice and it is not working. They don't know what else to do, and not knowing makes them feel out of control and fearful.

After people meet with us about managing their anger, they leave with many specific new choices and effective new tools. They can't wait to try them out on their jobs or at home with their spouses, their parents or their kids. They come back with reports of their successes and they want to know more, so we tell them. The more successes they have, the better their relationships become, and the better they feel about themselves.

That is the point of this book. We teach people how to use an anger situation to strengthen the most important and most overlooked relationship -- our relationship with ourselves. We learn to stop being afraid of our anger situation and to start seeing it as an opportunity to do something productive and constructive for both ourselves and our loved ones. We feel empowered, competent, in control, independent, mature, encouraged and confident. These are all facets of self-respect, which is our reward for an anger job well done.

In this work, we will introduce some of the specific anger management techniques that we use in the Chicago Anger Clinic. At first reading, you may, say to yourself, "Oh, this is too easy. This is too simplistic." If these techniques were as easy to use as they appear to be, you would have been using them for years. They are not easy, they only seem to be on the printed page.

The first problem in adapting these anger management techniques is the universal inertia that kicks in whenever we try anything new for the first time. It is so much cozier to perform the same old routines even when they have not worked for years. A second difficulty is that we may have impediments in our personal makeup that are inconsistent with these new approaches. We will try to identify some of these impediments for you as we go along. We will also provide you with the tools to help you grow, both personally and professionally.

Don't Fight the Feeling

When an old attitude such as, "It is my role in life to please others at my own expense," runs into a new technique, such as "Tell the Truth," the conflict becomes painfully apparent. You want to tell the truth, but you fear that the truth will be very displeasing and that you will not be able to find a rational compromise between the two warring attitudes in your heart.

We are letting you know in advance that we do not advocate open warfare between your contradictory attitudes. Do not fight the feeling. Instead, work carefully to replace one attitude with another over time, so that you can make conscious choices on an informed basis. We need not go head to head with ourselves, for we gradually outgrow that which needs to be outgrown. Replacing, choosing and outgrowing rather than fighting, are the preferred operations for implementing these techniques that we failed to acquire on our way into adulthood.

The Roots of Anger

Anger management techniques fall into two major categories -- good and bad. Good techniques make things better, while bad ones make them worse. Bad techniques include screaming, punching, swearing, sulking, cursing and hitting. Our use of these techniques does not mean that we are bad people. It may mean that we are just loyal, obedient students of the parental models who gave us these examples to follow.

Your choice of techniques may have something to do with your role in the family constellation. For example, if your older sister was a screamer, you were sure that you couldn't catch up to her in that arena, so you may have chosen to use sarcasm as your way of expressing your anger. If your baby brother had flaming temper tantrums that were worse than yours, you may have surrendered that technique to him and opted for the silent treatment as your way of heightening the contrast between your developing personhood and his.

Parental Models

Perhaps your parents were evenly matched sparring partners, and seemed to value solving problems by squaring off in the bedroom. You may have assumed that this was the technique of choice and you therefore carried this parental example over into your own adult relationships.

We learn anger management in the same way that we learn to wash dishes and make beds. There is not a whole lot of intellectual debate or rational discourse prior to the adoption of a mannerism that will last a lifetime. In other words, in the area of anger management, there hasn't been a brain cell working for four generations.

It is no wonder that we find ourselves in an ocean of insoluble social problems, including child abuse, spouse battering, granny bashing, runaway kids, drive-by shootings, racial tension, mass murder and labor strife. All of these problems arise out of the mismanagement of anger problems that may have been minor disruptions at one time, but have become major social problems now.

You would think that the social engineers, political experts and corporate tycoons would have long ago established institutes and academies for the study and improvement of anger management practices in this country. One reason that they have not is that *nice people like us, are not supposed to get angry in the first place. Anger is a "no, no." It isn't pleasant -- it's scary. We all like pleasant things and do not like scary things, except on the big screen where we know they will be under control. Therefore, why should we study an emotion that we aren't supposed to have? Why should we learn how to solve a problem that isn't supposed to exist?*

We cannot argue with that logic. It is not the logic of the grown-ups that we are now. It is the logic of the four year olds that we used to be and never outgrew. As long as we are the prisoners of this infantile logic, our anger problems -- which we aren't supposed to have but we do -- will get only worse. Anger problems will push husbands and wives to the brink of divorce and over the edge, disrupt business partnerships and inflame working relationships. They will impel young people into the whirlwind of self-destructive behavior. Our mangled anger patterns will stress our bodies with hypertension, ulcers and strokes. They will plunge us into depression, anxiety and suicidal impulses.

After our anger attack blows over, we will not understand why we did the things we did. We will say, "Something came over me," "It was a crime of passion," or "I killed her because I loved her." For a population that prides itself on its technological and medical accomplishments, these throwbacks to the Stone Age are an enduring disgrace.

The Anger Management Techniques

There are two kinds of anger management techniques -- the "good" kind and the "bad" kind. Most of the following anger management techniques are the "good" kind that we hope will make things better. But we also have thrown in a few of the "bad" kind so that if you recognize yourself, you can identify what you have been doing wrong all these years. Then, if you are so disposed, you can choose to replace your current counter-productive techniques with one or two that might make things better for you, your loved ones and the generations to come.

ANGER TERMS

Here are some of the major concepts that we use throughout this book:

Anger is not a weakness or a crime. It is merely unpleasant. We define anger *as an emotional response to a grievance.* The immediate grievance can be real or imaginary, but the anger itself is valid. We try to find the middle ground in managing our anger. Socrates called it, "the golden mean."

Our approach is to validate the person's anger first and save the questions about the grievance for later. Conducting an inquisition into the truth or falsity of the grievance when someone is in pain is a negative technique that we call, "the Perry Mason Syndrome."

The **gamut**. Many people believe that anger refers only to blowing one's stack. Anger runs the whole gamut from mild irritation to homicidal rage, even to World War III. It is all anger, whether we express it openly or not, and whether the grievance is real or imaginary. The emotional response takes place and it must be managed.

Mischief often makes us angry. We define mischief as *"that which does not need to be done."* When we learn how to recognize mischief and deal with it appropriately, we will not get so angry so often.

Good intentions make us angry, too. When people feel inadequately prepared to solve a problem, they make up a solution that sounds good at the time and proceed to inflict it upon us. We aren't supposed to protest because they "mean well." It is very frustrating. Good intentions are mischief. Like all mischief, they are self-indulgent, counterproductive and ultimately self-destructive.

We can learn to replace our own inappropriate good intentions with *real intentions*, which means doing what reality requires us to do, no more and no less. We must be able to perceive what is required of us. We must use our adult judgment to determine what to do about it, and we must have the courage to do what needs to be done.

Courage is the willingness to take a risk. Our adult judgment tells us which risks are worth taking.

Super-anger means feeling angrier than the situation requires us to feel. We understand the excess anger as arising from a perceived similarity between the current situation and an unresolved anger problem from the past.

Frustration is a compound emotion. It consists of feeling angry plus powerless and out of control.

The **anger roles** that we play in the present originated in childhood. We have carried them into adulthood with us. We can use an anger situation to actively replace our role as Victim, Pleaser, Rebel, Scapegoat and so on with a mature identity of our own.

An attitude is a predisposition to behave in a certain way. We don't even have to think about it. We have attitudes about our anger that get us in trouble that could have been avoided. We can learn to identify these attitudes and replace them with more appropriate ones.

Homework is the name that we have given to the act of replacing our old attitudes with new ones. When life gives us an opportunity to change our way of responding, we actively choose to shift our gears, and we choose to behave in the new way that we have learned. For example, we use one of the anger management techniques. We are taking an appropriate action on our own legitimate terms in our own behalf. We are not making mischief, we are doing what needs to be done. That is a homework.

Catch yourself is one of the techniques for remembering to do your homework. You see a situation as an opportunity to do something that you have never done before. You are about to react in the old way and you choose not to. You have *caught yourself in the act*. You are free to make new choices. It takes courage, but the reward is worth it.

Absurd attitudes. Some attitudes from childhood are absurd, but we do not have words for them in our language. For instance, it is absurd for an intelligent person to feel stupid if he forgets his mother-in-law's birthday, or his boss's wife's name. An appropriately absurd name for this predisposition to call ourselves and each other stupid is "stupiditude." We cannot respect stupidity in ourselves or others, but "stupiditude" is an absurd, but acceptable human imperfection.

Another word that we use is **rationalitosis**, which is the absurd delusion that the person you are talking to is in his right mind -- and vice versa. It includes the notion that we can solve every problem rationally to the third decimal place. Emotional problems need to be solved subjectively by replacing one set of feelings and attitudes with another. This cannot be done with a calculator.

Self-respect. In our anger therapy, we use an anger situation as an opportunity to grow. Specifically, we change the way we express our anger or respond to the anger of a loved one. In that moment we are changed. Our self-doubt, even self-contempt has been replaced by something better: self-respect. We have earned it. After a few such accomplishments, or "homeworks," our periods of self-respect start to run together. We are no longer our parents' inadequate, inferior child. We are a *worthwhile human being in spite of our faults and imperfections.*

Suppression means stifling our anger because we are afraid to express it openly.

Repression refers to anger that has been pushed below the level of conscious awareness because it is too dangerous to deal with, or even remember.

Anger fears. We have learned to be afraid of our anger. We are afraid that if we express our anger openly, we will be victimized, abandoned, even annihilated. We spend our lives and energies trying to prevent these things from happening.

Control. In order to prevent these negative consequences, we institute a system of control when we are still a young child. We teach ourselves to express our anger in ways that are safe, but which do not give us any real relief from the emotional pressure. We define control as if it meant "preventing bad, scary things from happening to us." This is an immature definition. It sets us up to control in crazy ways that can only work in reverse. We will feel out of control most of the time. A better definition of control is *taking life as it comes and doing the best we can with it.* That is what self-respecting people do.

Anxiety is the feeling that the bad thing is going to happen any minute. When our anger is out of control, we are out of control. We experience this out-of-control anger as anxiety.

Panic is the feeling that the bad thing is happening to us right now and that we are going to die. We feel totally out of control.

Early recollections. The early recollections that we use in this book are not dramatic or sensational. They did not cause the individual's problems in later life. We are interested in why someone remembers these events for thirty or more years. It is because these recollections reveal the attitudes about the self, others and life that the individual acquired in childhood. For example, "I am a victim," "People are out to get me," and "Life is scary and dangerous." These built in attitudes predispose us to be scared and angry even when there is no basis for these feelings in the real world. These attitudes are often mistaken and they interfere with our coping in the present. They are often negative and preclude a happy, successful passage through life. If these mistaken attitudes can be held up to the individual for what they are, a child's misperceptions and misconstrusions, there is the possibility that they can be discarded and replaced with attitudes that conform to the realities in which we find ourselves. If we can make that replacement, the probabilities of our achieving happiness and success will be increased.

Problem solving. Life presents us with problems every time we turn around. As children, we did not know how to solve problems. We remember our humiliating failures and the painful consequences of our ineptitude. We took these failures personally, as if they were a reflection on our worth as a person. We acquired feelings and attitudes about problems that were exaggerated and scary. We bring these carryovers from the past to our problems in the present, where they interfere with our functioning. One such attitude is, "Life is pleasant for me when I can solve problems; it is very unpleasant for me when I cannot." The problem itself is not the issue now, the problem is the way we feel about the problem and about ourselves as people in the world. We can learn how to put ourselves on a basis of self-respect which will make us much less vulnerable to taking the ups and downs of life as personally as we used to when we were five years old. We will be free to solve more problems than ever before.

Pain. Pain creates problems for us that we do not know how to solve. We want to relieve our pain, but we never learned how to give ourselves emotional first aid. We have good intentions for ourselves which only make things worse.

Making the situation more complicated is the fact that we do not know what our pain is. Self-contempt, for instance, is a pain that we all feel to a greater or lesser degree. We try to relieve it by overcompensating and making either fools or tyrants of ourselves. We lose either way, and so do our loved ones. Or we try to numb our pain by escaping into drugs, alcohol, sex, gambling and other negative excitements.

Anger is painful, too. We try to relieve this pain by displacing our anger onto an innocent party, or rationalizing it away such as, "He didn't really mean it," or other inappropriate techniques that we picked up in grade school.

Since these pain-relieving techniques do not really work, the pain does not go away. We may have pushed it below the level of conscious awareness, but it is still there. We now have a pain that we cannot feel, a pain that ruins our happiness without our even knowing that it is down there. That is a problem that very few of us know how to solve all by ourselves.

Overcompensation is the process of trying to prove that we are not worthless and inferior. This is our "solution" to the problem of feeling "not good enough." Since it works in reverse, we wind up confirming our self-contempt in the end. We feel compelled to keep trying forever. Mischief often comes from this attempt to prove something that cannot be proved. We try too hard. We make up good intentions that make no sense in the real world. The real antidote to our painful feelings of worthlessness is to replace them with feelings of self-respect by doing homework that needs to be done.

Enough. Unself-respecting people cannot feel good enough. They cannot feel smart enough, pretty enough, thin enough, successful enough or strong enough. Their overcompensatory striving to achieve "enoughness" can only make things worse. When we do our homework, we feel competent enough, responsible enough, smart enough and worthwhile enough. We have earned the right to feel that *"as good as we are right now, that is good enough. If we are better still next week, that is all right, too."*

This is not a prescription for stagnation or smug self-satisfaction. Self-respect gives us the freedom to do what is in us to do. Self-respecting people have no intention of vegetating -- it would be inconsistent with their self-respect.

Emotional First Aid. We can learn how to identify our pain and call it by its rightful name. This is a first step toward relieving it in the right way. We can learn how to catch ourselves about to overreact and choose not to. We can validate our loved one's pain and find that we have relieved our own. We can choose to express our anger like a mature adult for a change, and experience feelings of relief, control, security, identity and all the other facets of self-respect. We can learn how to disengage from mischief.

Disengage from mischief. Perhaps the most potent remedy in our emotional first aid kit is our power to disengage from mischief. As soon as we have identified someone's negative, provocative behavior as mischief, we enable ourselves to do something about it. We are empowered to do the unexpected. Instead of defending, protesting, explaining or cajoling, which are all good intentions, we can choose to have a real intention for ourselves. We can use our adult judgment to tell us what the situation really requires us to do, and then we do it. Sometimes the situation requires us to do nothing.

Vignette: Mutual Mischief

Sarah was upstairs in the shower. She heard three-year-old Bradley, crying, and thirty three-year-old Larry, trying to talk him out of it. He was saying, "If you can't tell me why you are crying, then you shouldn't be crying." In the old days, before the Anger Clinic, Sarah would have been out of that shower, into her robe and down those stairs in 6.5 seconds flat. This time was different. She had had the course and she applied what she had learned to the real world. She decided not to run down there and give Larry another useless lecture on the absurdity of his logic, or to scoop up the child and rescue him from his inadequately prepared father. She decided to let go of her self-assigned responsibility to solve every family problem perfectly and instantly. She realized that the old way never changed anything. It hadn't helped anyone.

For the first time in her life, Sarah consciously and deliberately chose to do nothing. She let it go. She went on with her shower. The crying and yelling stopped much sooner than it would have in the past.

Sarah had disengaged from the mischief in the kitchen. These two people, without knowing it, were used to putting on a show for mom. They expected her to come down and react to it. It didn't need to be done. Sarah chose not to be a part of their mutual mischief. She arranged to live on her own appropriate terms for a little while. It felt good. She didn't feel guilty of the crime of negligence or irresponsibility, she didn't feel out of control, she felt in control of herself. She had spared her husband and child the pain of an out of control, super-angry, super-counterproductive mother from hell. She had made it happen. No one had to know about it but her. She felt that she had assumed appropriate responsibility and allowed both Larry to learn from his own mistakes and Bradley to solve his own interpersonal relationship problems. He was going to need the practice.

Sarah had given herself "Emotional First Aid." She had replaced her good intention to "rescue" her child with a real intention -- to let them work it out for themselves. This was not selfish, it was appropriate behavior. It deprived these mischief makers of their negative payoff. She had experienced the facets of self-respect. She had used an anger situation to move from a felt minus (self-doubt) to a felt plus (self-respect). She had set an example of appropriate responsibility and admirable restraint for her loved ones to see and follow. She had solved the problem in the right way. She had healed herself.

"The unexamined life is not worth living."

Socrates

#1. ABANDONMENT

We rarely experience anger in its purest state. Our anger in the present is often "contaminated" by remembrances of angers past that have never been dealt with properly. As children, we did not know how to manage them properly, so we mismanaged them. We did not get relief from them at the time, so they are still circulating down there below the level of our conscious awareness. When something in the present reminds us of an anger from the past, we often become angrier than we need to be. This is called, "super-anger." For example, when our wife, Doris, does not come home at the time she said she would, it makes us angry. If it "reminds" us of an abandonment that we experienced in our early childhood, our anger in the present is reinforced. We experience the overwhelming feeling that we are being abandoned all over again, which of course we are not. When Doris finally does come home, we aren't relieved to see her safe and sound, we are angry at her for causing us this unnecessary pain and grief.

Our anger management technique is to identify the contaminant from the past, so that we can put it into a more realistic perspective in the present. When we are angry, we should remember that we do not want to go through this agony again. We have a choice now that we did not have before. We can remind ourselves to ask a focusing question such as, *"Wait a minute. I am not 'upset,' I am angry. What angers me the most? Is it that Doris is 47 minutes late?"* Very often the answer from the past will pop into our consciousness. "I feel alone and abandoned, just like I felt when I was a kid." We may have a recollection of a terrified child pressing his nose to the cold window pane waiting for the headlights of a car pulling into the driveway. We can say to ourselves, *"That was then and this is now. I am an independent grown-up, now. I have a personhood of my own that I did not have as a child. I have adult resources. I have choices and I have me. I cannot be abandoned. I can be angry at Doris for being late, but that is manageable. I will tell her that I am angry at her for not calling me, but I am glad to see her."*

THE ABANDONED CHILD

"I am abandoned forever and it's my fault for not being good enough."

#2. ABUSE

One of the most prevalent anger mismanagement techniques in America today is abuse. We have an epidemic of abuse in this country including: wife abuse, husband abuse, child abuse, sibling abuse, teacher abuse, student abuse, employee abuse, elder abuse and drug abuse. If there is one thing that we abuse more than substances, it is each other. How do we understand abuse as a social phenomenon? Is it a reflection of the proliferation of television violence? We had abuse before television was invented. Is it a reflection of hard economic times? We have had abuse in good times, too. Is it a matter of "low self-esteem?" People who profess to have "high self-esteem" abuse each other, too. Is abuse an urban phenomenon? No, for we have abuse surrounding us everywhere.

Under what circumstances are abusers provoked to inflict pain on their fellow human beings?

When they have a problem that they cannot solve;

When they are not getting what they want;

When they have "a hard day;"

When they are not appreciated;

When they are inconvenienced;

When they are feeling victimized;

When they feel out of control;

When they have suffered a loss;

When they do not receive "proper" respect.

All of the above circumstances are actually grievances. We all have grievances, but a major characteristic of abusers is that they do not manage their grievances very well. When we peel their "anger artichoke" down, we find that these grievances are not the real issue, they are only the occasion for the real issues which are hidden farther down. For example, these people feel inadequate to cope with the ups and downs of everyday life. When life or a loved one presents them with a problem that they cannot solve instantly and perfectly, as they require themselves to do, their preexisting feelings of inadequacy to cope are ignited and they explode.

The Issue Is Not the Issue

When abusers try to justify their hurtful behavior by screaming, "I just want to teach you a lesson," or "It's for your own good," these excuses are not to be taken at face value. It is ironic that they are abusing their victims with the "best of intentions." When they say, "You made me do this," or "You make me so mad," the purpose here is not to convey the truth about their motivation. These are all self-serving, self-deceiving cover stories. The abusers are trying to put the guilt and blame on the person being abused and very often they succeed. They arrange to have it both ways -- they can indulge themselves and it is never their fault. These are not valid explanations to be taken at face value, but a smokescreen behind which the abuser can operate in safety.

Abusers will say, by way of explanation, "That's just the way I am." What they are really saying is, "I have no interest in changing for you or anyone else. Take it or leave it. Don't say that I didn't warn you." They may seek to justify their abuse by claiming, "I'm under too much pressure." We are all under pressure. Self-respecting people take the trouble to learn how to manage the pressures of everyday life. What the abusers are really saying is, "I am inadequate to cope with life like other people and I have no intention of doing anything about my inadequacies. I expect you to do something about them and when you fail to achieve the perfection I require, that causes me a grievance. I have the right to complain about the service, even to punish you for disappointing me."

Many therapists focus on the abuser's overt behavior. They say, "You've got a temper. You've got to control that temper," as if abusers were interested in giving up an anger technique that has been successful all these years. Practitioners often consign abusers to self-help groups where they can exchange "war stories" with their fellow abusers, forever feeling sorry for their "misunderstood" selves all the while.

There are many more such surface "issues." Many of us stop looking right there and take these phony issues at face value as if they made sense. We debate with the abuser as if we could make him understand the error of his ways.

But there are deeper issues that underlie all of these surface considerations. Most of us experience these negative situations but we do not abuse each other when we do. We do not use these disappointments and grievances as an excuse to inflict pain on a "safe" target. Abusers never pick an unsafe target. They are mean, but they aren't stupid. What do we non-abusers have that abusers do not have and do not even wish to attain if they could? What are the real issues?

The answer to this question is twofold:

1.   The first issue is anger. All of these negative situations make us angry. Some of us have learned how to manage our anger during our childhood or in therapy as adults. Abusers, on the other hand, do not know how to manage their anger in appropriate, civilized ways and many of them are not interested in learning how. So they mismanage it. They express their anger in destructive ways that can only make the situation

worse. They do not learn from their repetitive experiences. Often, there is no negative consequence from which they can draw a constructive conclusion. Even when there is a consequence, it may not scratch where they itch. They miss the point of it and repeat their offensive behavior anyway.

2. The second issue is that abusers hold themselves in contempt. It follows that they can only have contempt for those who love them. Their abusive behavior is a derivative of their contempt for themselves. Their self-destructive behavior is consistent with their feelings that they are worthless and undeserving of happiness and success. We can not reason them out of their negative attitudes towards themselves and others. The newspapers often say that a particular case of abuse was senseless -- we see now that sense has nothing to do with it.

The combination of these two factors, mismanaged, out-of-control anger, in a context of self-contempt, are the real issues. They predispose abusers to behave in ways that they do not understand or even *want* to understand. Their anger and self-contempt are painful, and abusing others is how they relieve their pain. This is how they solve problems that they feel inadequately prepared to solve otherwise. Unfortunately for them and for us, the catch is that they are relieving nothing and solving nothing. The pain will be back tomorrow and the problems will be worse than they were before.

Some of us try to make these people understand the error of their ways. Our mistake is to think that they are just like us, just regular folks who need a little helping hand to make them see the light. They are not like us. We need to stop trying to help these people out until we find out what the real issues are.

At the Anger Clinic, one of the first steps in our

therapeutic approach is to help abusers learn the underlying purposes of their abusive behavior. For instance, their purpose may be:

1. To get attention, even if it is negative. To them, it is better than no attention at all. Attention validates that they exist. They cannot validate their own existence.

2. To gain power over others. Not so they can use this power in positive, constructive ways, which they do not know how to do, but so that they can reduce the pain of their powerlessness. Their pain makes them totally self-preoccupied. They do not care about others. What is worse, they *cannot* care about others.

3. To get revenge on people who have caused them a grievance, even if the grievance is imaginary, fictitious or a misperception. The pain of the grievance is real and it must be relieved by hurting others in the name of "equity" and "fair play."

4. To drive people away from them so that they can withdraw from life into a cocoon of discouragement. That is how they hope to keep from failing even more in the future.

Their loved ones may mean well, for they do want to help. However, they do not understand the abuser's underlying anger and self-contempt. Their good intentions can only make things worse. The abuser will beat them until they give up and stop trying to help. When they do, they will lose and the abuser will win. Our goal is to replace these negative purposes with positive ones. We do this by giving appropriate homework to do as you will soon see.

Another step in the healing process is to find out how the abuser got this way. We do this by asking a focusing question such as, *"What is the first thing you remember from your childhood?"*

Vignette: Victim or Victimizer?

Ron was an abuser. His wife divorced him because of his cruelty to her and the children. He has not learned a thing from the experience. He is now abusing his new girl friend, Sylvia. He is in danger of losing her, too. He came in for counseling because she insisted. He doesn't think he needs it.

Ron's first early recollection was of his father forcing him into a corner of his room and beating him with a rolled up newspaper. Our investigation does not end with the finding that Ron was an abused child. We wish to identify the specific conclusions, attitudes and expectations that Ron derived from this experience.

Using the limited insight of a five-year-old child, these are some of the lessons that Ron learned on that day that his father beat him. He has never unlearned them:

1. "I must have done something wrong. Wrongness is to be punished violently."

2. "Control is used for inflicting punishment on persons weaker than oneself."

3. "I am a victim, I am weak."

4. "My father is a victimizer, he is strong. He can do as he pleases. I would much rather be a victimizer than a victim."

5. "The only time my father pays attention to me is when he beats me. At least it proves I am alive."

6. "I cannot cope. I cannot solve my problems. When I can't solve problems in the present, it reminds me how weak and inadequate I really am. I do not want people to find out my secret inadequacy. I must control them in order to prevent that. I must be stronger than they are."

7. "My father solved his problems by beating people. If it's good enough for him, it's good enough for me."

One intervention that worked with Ron focused on his tendency to go into his victim role whenever he had a grievance. For instance, when Sylvia tried to defend herself against him, Ron perceived her behavior as an attack on him, a victimization. He hates to be victimized, especially by someone who is physically weaker than he is. He cannot permit that to happen. His only method of relieving the pain of his victimization was to become the victimizer. He was able to stop her "attack" by doing to her what his father did to him.

We agreed that Ron felt victimized by Sylvia's behavior. No one had ever agreed with him before. He had always been told that he had to understand the other person's distress. No one ever tried to understand him. That just compounded his feeling that he was a victim.

After validating Ron's perception of himself as the "innocent" victim of Sylvia's wrath, we said, "*Could it be, Ron, that you are perceiving victimization where no victimization is intended?*" We are not invalidating him, we are merely asking a question. Even if Ron says "no," which is not necessarily the truth, we have at least introduced to him the concept that perceptions can be mistaken and that it is all right to make mistakes. He will not be beaten for his "wrongness." We have created an atmosphere in which it is possible for Ron to accept his imperfection, which no one ever created for him before. He can begin to consider the possibility that he is not life's perpetual victim at all, but that he is a worthwhile human being in spite of his faults and imperfections.

Ron's homework is to see Sylvia not as a victimizer like his father, but as an imperfect human being, herself. She is not "wrong" and he is not "right." They are both imperfect human beings who make each other angry from time to time. Anger is not to be feared anymore. Ron is not seven years old. He can learn to say, *"It makes me angry when you do that, Sylvia."* He has a choice now that his father did not have. He can also learn to validate Sylvia's anger by saying, *"I'm sorry you are so angry."* That is what self-respecting people do.

Ron did his homework the next day. Sylvia did not understand something he said. She asked him to repeat it. In the old days, Ron would have felt "controlled" by her, like an inferior person about to be victimized. He would have taken her request personally, as if it were a reflection on his worth as a person, as if she were "blaming" him for not speaking clearly. He would have become angry and abusive in "self-defense." He chose not to. He just repeated what he had said. He had chosen to cooperate with her as an equal member of the human race. He had never seen an example of cooperation between his father and mother. He had become his own model -- he made it happen; it was his choice. He felt in control of himself, and that he had used mature judgment. He had an identity of his own to replace his old role as his father's terrified, inadequate victim. His homework had earned him the right to respect himself as an independent human being in his own right.

That night, Sylvia tied up the telephone for an hour. He wanted her attention and he wasn't getting it. This "grievance" made him angry. He was feeling victimized again. Ron gave himself the choice of expressing his anger the "new way" or the "old way." He chose the new way. He said, *"Sylvia, it makes me angry when you tie up the phone so long."* She said, "You're right. I'm sorry." There was no explosion of anger, no defensiveness, no name calling. Ron didn't miss the excitement of the bad old days. He felt relieved, liberated, calm and at peace with himself. These are all facets of self-respect.

The more homework Ron does, the more he replaces his self-contempt with self-respect. The more adequate Ron feels to cope with life, the less he needs to express his anger with his fists.

Some abusers are not ready to make these difficult transitions. They only do what is easy. That way, they cannot fail. Perhaps they have not suffered enough and cannot see why they should change at all. They think that their way of living is working. They are not paying any price for their misdeeds, but their loved ones are. They cannot see why they should quit when they are winning.

Do's and Don'ts:

Do not attack or defend on the abuser's terms. You can choose to behave on your own valid terms.

The issue is not what the abuser is complaining about; the issue is anger.

Use a focusing question to help the abuser identify the real source of his pain. *"What happened to make you so angry?"*

Validate the abuser's anger. *"I'm sorry you are so angry. I'd be angry too, if that happened to me."*

Identify the "victim" component of the abuser's distress. *"I'll bet you felt like a victim when that happened."*

You can even say, *"I didn't mean to make you feel like a victim."*

"I am not your enemy. I am on your side."

#3. ACTIVE REMORSE

Active remorse does not mean feeling guilty for what you did and buying her a fur coat to cover your tracks, or baking a batch of his favorite cookies. It does not mean brooding forever over your sins of omission and commission. It means using your adult judgment to determine an appropriate course of remedial action. Sometimes it means saying, *"I'm sorry."* You may never have said I'm sorry in your life. You didn't want to give anyone the satisfaction. Maybe it is time you did.

On other occasions, active remorse may mean actually spending money to buy a replacement. Some of us are willing to go as high as two bucks. Grown-ups are prepared to go as high as the reality of the situation requires them to go. If we do not know what the injured party wants us to do, we can ask something like, *"What remedy do you seek?"* This is not abject submission; this is cooperation.

#4. ADMIRABLE RESTRAINT

Some people express too much anger, while others express too little. Very few people express their anger right down the middle between the two extremes and get the relief that they need to get.

Sometimes, it is not possible or practical to express your anger openly. On these occasions, managing your anger means riding it out, keeping your feelings to yourself and resisting the often powerful temptation to "let 'er rip," which takes no brains at all.

When you exercise "Admirable Restraint," you are not suppressing your anger below the level of conscious awareness or rationalizing it away such as, "Oh, he doesn't really mean what he is saying," or "He can't help himself." You are fully aware of the fire in your belly. You are making wide awake choices in the real world and using your adult judgment to determine your behavior at every point.

You are not doing it for the other person; you are doing it for you. You know what the consequences will be if you let fly and you are consciously choosing to spare yourself this unnecessary fallout. You are not taking the other person's mischief personally or literally. You are managing your anger and your life competently as a self-respecting human being should do under combat conditions. You are not fighting harder; you are fighting smarter.

#5. AFFIRM LIFE

When our anger gets the better of us and ferments into vindictiveness, depression, discouragement and despair, the oil in our lamp burns very low. Our energy is bound up in negative emotions and there is not much left for us. That is when we are tempted to chuck it all, crawl in our hole and hibernate until spring.

Many of us give in to this temptation, until, after a while, our hibernations seem to run together and life has passed us by. It was the only one we had.

Self-respecting people use a technique called "Affirming Life." They have a choice that their vegetating neighbors do not have. They can choose to manage their anger properly and keep it from turning into such emotional symptoms as depression, anxiety and paranoia, and they can get back in the flow. It is hard to do, but they know that the other way is even harder.

Here is an example of how we can make appropriate anger choices in the moment that we are angry.

Vignette: Shifting Gears

Julie and Jim were engaged. Jim wanted to buy a brand new stereo set that they would both enjoy. He read all the catalogues and magazines until he found one that really filled the bill. He took Julie downtown to see it in the store. He couldn't wait to see her reaction.

"Is that the one?" she said. "It's so bulky. I thought it would be smaller. Don't they have it in blonde mahogany? This is so dark. Don't they have anything else?"

Jim could feel the old pulling in his gut. He had learned to recognize that pulling as his organism's anger response to a grievance. He wasn't exactly sure what the grievance was. It angered him that his beloved did not share his taste in acoustical hardware, but more than that, he felt that his hours of research in this field were insignificant and unappreciated. He felt "good for nothing" and invalidated.

They had planned to go to dinner afterward at their special restaurant on the waterfront. Jim felt sick to his stomach and had no appetite for dinner now. He felt like going back to his apartment and dozing off. That was when he remembered his choices: He could choose to withdraw from life as he did all through college when the going got rough, or he could allow himself to be angry at Julie for her lack of consideration for his feelings and her failure to appreciate his expertise. He chose not to take Julie's preferences in den furniture personally and not to get angry at himself for "allowing" the disappointment to happen. He was still angry, but he was managing it like a grown-up. He shifted his emotional gears, explained his preferences to Julie in language she could almost understand and made his purchase.

He was still angry as he left the store, walked to the car and steered toward the restaurant. Julie began talking about other things, never realizing how close she came to having canned tuna for dinner that night, while Jim found himself involved once again in the human race. His anger dissipated, as it had before when he had remembered to manage it correctly. It seemed to him that it was dissipating sooner each time.

He had voted against withdrawing into his hurt feelings, which he knew was a prescription for a solitary, joyless existence. Instead, he had affirmed life on his own valid terms.

#6. AGREE WITH IT

This technique is a specific example of Technique #20, "Do the Unexpected." When your provokers are venting their anger, taunting you with nonsense that they will probably regret in the morning, you can defuse their unreasonable, non-subjective emotionality by finding something in their tirade to agree with. Here are some game-enders:

Provocation	Disagreeing, (Defending/ Explaining)	Agreeing
"I've never seen a mess like this."	"You're always complaining."	*"It's awful, isn't it?"*
"Can't you do anything right?"	"I do plenty of things right, but you never notice."	*"I sure blew it this time, didn't I?"*
"Your mother is driving me crazy."	"You never liked my mother, admit it."	*"She sure has her ups and downs, doesn't she?"*

We are not agreeing that they are right, only that they feel the way they feel. We are letting them know that we have no intention of trying to talk them out of it or of defending our integrity or anyone else's. Neither do we have any intention of making useless countermischief on their terms. They cannot take away our self-respect. This response costs us nothing. It takes the wind out of their sails. They cannot fight with agreement.

#7. BLAMING

When we are angry, we are in pain. One of our first priorities is to relieve our pain as fast as we can. We want fast, fast, fast relief. We imagine that we can solve our problem by:

1. Identifying the culprit who caused our pain.

2. Transferring our pain to the offender in a way that will give us gratification. The pleasure of this gratification, we hope, will assuage the pain of our anger.

3. Distracting others from our own contribution to our present distress.

We imagine that we are proceeding in a rational, logical manner when we point fingers of guilt, shame, fault and blame, but we are not. This entire operation is born of emotion, and our intellectual faculties are just going along for the ride.

An emotion is a feeling that impels us to move. When we feel angry sitting on the sofa, we are not doing anything about it. It is not an emotion, but a feeling. However, when our anger energizes us to track down the miscreant who left the skateboard on the basement stairs, that is an emotion. We are seeking relief from the pressure, tension and stress that this emotion is causing us. We are behaving according to attitudes that we learned when we were four years old, if not earlier: "Find the one who did it and do it back worse." Our reasoning is equally immature: "If you cause me pain, I have the right to cause you pain in return.

31

That's fair." This is not the logic of a mature adult. These attitudes are out of our conscious control.

When we blame someone, we are inflicting the pain of guilt which we hope is commensurate with the degree of pain that was caused us. When we dump guilt, we are at the same time tearing down the alleged offender's self-respect. Even young children know that guilty people are worthless; and that is how they come to feel worthless. The issue is no longer guilt or innocence, it is the fact of the accusation itself that turns their self-respect to self-contempt. Even when the child is exonerated, the scar of that accusation remains behind. The damage has been done. If the accusation is correct, the children do not learn from their mistakes. They take the accusation personally, as a reflection on their worth as a person. The child is "wrong." There is no appeal to a higher court for successful defense, there are only unsuccessful ones. There is no cure for being "wrong."

A better technique than blaming, guilting, ridiculing, fault-finding and criticizing would be to tell the truth. That is the last thing we think of doing. We think that the truth lies in unmasking the perpetrator, even if it is a hapless child or a well-intentioned spouse. But that is not the truth -- the truth is that there was a grievance and the grievance made us angry. Our pain is real and we need to relieve it in ways that work. We can choose to say, *"It makes me very angry when you leave things on the stairs that cause me to slide all the way down into the basement."* That is a powerful, impressive statement. Children can understand that our anger is a logical consequence of their not picking things up. Our anger is not a wipeout of their personhood. We are only saying that what happened made us angry. We are making a distinction between the deed and the doer. They are worthwhile in spite of what happened, and so are we. Blaming is not a logical consequence of anything. It is an illogical, destructive consequence.

Do's and Don'ts:

Do not take your blamer's mischief personally as a reflection of your worth as a person.

Do not defend, debate or rebut the substance of the blame. It is only mischief.

Do not try to make sense out of nonsense.

Things to do instead:

"Thank you for calling this to my attention."

"I know you are doing this for my own good and I appreciate it, but I will be fine."

"How does that help?"

The Wimp Factor

Some people have major conflicts with the "Agree With It" technique. They have never agreed with anyone and they are not about to start now. It would be "wimpy" and they couldn't live with themselves. "Real" grown-ups stand up for their rights; only "wimps" are agreeable.

Their definition of "wimp" is one that they acquired in the early stages of their personal development. To a four year old, people are either weak or strong, right or wrong. There is no middle ground between the two extremes. To this day, they cannot compromise with their immature, self-indulgent definitions of themselves as people in the world. These are some of their impediments to agreeing with their fellow human beings:

1. They take what other individuals say personally. They then feel compelled to defend their threatened personhood at the other person's expense.

2. They take what is said literally, as if it made sense. Most of the time, it is only nonsense intended to provoke a negative reaction, which it does. They are going to fall for it every time.

3. They confuse agreement with submission and inferiority. They cannot allow themselves to be inferior to anyone.

4. They stand in judgment on other people's nonsense and find them guilty. They are wrong. They cannot agree with wrongness; they can only agree with rightness. Since they are the only one who is ever right, they can only agree with themselves.

5. They feel that it is their responsibility to teach people the error of their ways. They cannot do that by agreeing with error.

6. They feel that it is up to them to make wrongdoers understand the truth. They would feel guilty if they failed to keep trying to make them understand their version of the truth.

7. They have played the role of the Oppositional Child all their lives. They define themselves by contrasting themselves with everyone else. They are not really *for* themselves, they are just *against* others.

The irony is that people who can retain their composure under these anger attacks are not wimps at all. They are showing resolute competence under fire. They are not reacting to these negative stimuli like laboratory rats; they are using their adult judgment to make appropriate choices under difficult circumstances. They are showing their independence, individuality and their strength of character by doing the unexpected on their own valid terms.

Some people admire aggressiveness under all circumstances. To the aggressive person who feels like a hammer, every problem is a nail. But some problems are not nails. They require a degree of flexibility and accommodation. That is not wimpiness, but self-respect. It is a sad reflection on our contemporary way of life that we value the mindless, "spunky" counterattack over a thoughtful, stress-relieving intervention.

Agreeing with what the other person says is not to be confused with appeasement, placating or kowtowing. Those are all forms of wimping out. The self-respecting person is merely agreeing that these other people feel the way they feel at the time. They may feel differently tomorrow. We can agree with them tomorrow, too. Here are some more examples:

"People are no damn good."

"It seems that way, doesn't it?"

"Nobody likes me."

"It's very lonesome, isn't it?"

"I can beat up anyone in the joint."

"You certainly can."

It costs us nothing to let these other people know that we heard what they said. We are also letting them know that we have no intention of letting them manipulate us into defending the opposite point of view. We have no such responsibility to correct another human being's world view or to debate their nonsense as if it made sense. As self-respecting grown-ups, we have the power of choice. We can choose to let it go and say something appropriate that is conciliatory. We do not make things worse. Our goal is to make things better. It is written, "A soft answer turneth away wrath" -- we are still having a hard time believing it.

#8. THE ANGER LETTER

One way to solve an "insoluble" anger problem is to write our anger down on a piece of paper. This, too, seems too easy to be of any use. Yet, this technique is very successful if we do it in the right way. We are not writing a hate letter or a laundry list of complaints and criticisms. We are directing our specific angers toward another entity outside of ourself.

1. Writing our abstract feelings and attitudes down on a piece of paper makes them tangible and concrete before our very eyes. We cannot manage abstract thoughts about our life or about ourselves. However, we can begin to evaluate and sort them out when we see them in black and white in front of us.

2. Writing our thoughts and feelings down can begin a process of association that brings up ideas from the past that are not accessible otherwise. Seeing these ideas before us now through adult eyes gives us a chance to evaluate them as we might not have otherwise. If we see that they are no more than childhood misperceptions, we can choose to replace them with more appropriate ideas and attitudes.

3. Writing is an action in the real world. When we take this overt action, it gives rise to psychological, biochemical and physiological responses that brooding or intending cannot evoke.

4. Writing is a choice that we have made. The power of choice is in itself a welcome antidote to the miserable feeling that "there is nothing I can do about it." We have given ourselves the feeling that there is something we can do about our anger and we are doing it. The power of choice liberates us from our frustration -- the feeling of anger, powerlessness and loss of control.

These letters do not have to be mailed. That is optional. We are not writing the letter to enlighten the other person. We are doing it to give ourself some timely relief from our own distress. If we are angry at a deceased loved one, at God, at life, at the system or even at ourself, we can write our anger down. Afterwards, we can file our letter, tear it up or burn it -- that is our choice, too.

This technique even works with children. They, too, should be encouraged to express their anger appropriately, even if it is at us. They are not saying, "I hate you," only that we caused them a grievance whether it is real or imaginary, and it made them angry. If they are too young to write a letter, they can draw a picture (see #24, Draw a Picture).

#9. CATCH YOURSELF IN THE ACT

Most of your present anger management techniques are no more than bad habits that you picked up along the way and never outgrew. Now you can. You can use an anger situation to begin the process of replacing these old habits with some less offensive new ones. The first step is to be aware that you have these inappropriate carryovers from your childhood. Whether you are using sarcasm, revenge, sulking, the silent treatment, hitting, wall-banging or other negative means, your homework is to catch yourself in the act of doing it and then choose not to. You can choose to stop it at any time. With practice, you will catch yourself sooner each time and, therefore, stop sooner. You can choose to replace your inappropriate, relationship-killing habit with one or more of the new techniques in this book.

Someday, you will be able to catch yourself before you start. That's "bingo." That is self-respect.

"When I was young, I wanted to be somebody, but I guess I should have been more specific. "

Lily Tomlin & Jane Wagner
The Search For Intelligent Life In The Universe
1986, Harper Collins, NY, NY

#10. COMMUNICATING IN A NEW KEY

You do not realize it, but you are communicating in different keys all day long. You use one key for your spouse, another for your two-year-old daughter, yet another for your boss and still another for your racquetball buddies. Often, you change from one key to another instantly -- for instance, when you pick up the telephone in the middle of a fight. You do it without being consciously aware of it. It would be useful if you could learn to do it in the middle of an anger attack.

Some keys are scary, unpleasant and anger provoking, "*Do this! Do that! Jump when I tell you!*" This is the *imperative voice*. We are not even aware that we are using it half of the time. This key is not taken kindly by your hearers. They become testy and rebel against you or they become intimidated by you and resentfully submit to your tyranny. Neither response is conducive to happy relationships. People tend to resent being torn down to bolster your shaky ego. They are not favorably impressed by your imperiousness. They are negatively impressed, which to you is better than not being impressed at all.

You can choose to modulate your tone into one that encourages cooperation between equals. You may have to practice, just like when you were learning to play the saxophone. If you do not know how it is done, look around you and listen. There are people around you who are securing cooperation all the time. Listen to the tone they use, listen to their "music." Watch what they do. Instead of saying, "Why can't I ever get any help around here?" which is merely mismanaged anger, some of them choose to say, "*I would like your help over here.*" That has the advantage of offering the other person the choice of helping you or not. If you do it in the right key, they often make the right choice. You will often find that the music you choose is more important than the words!

"Some people can resist anything but temptation. "

Rudolph Dreikurs

Another key that you do not need is the accusatory voice such as, "Why did you do that? Why are you so stupid?" This is not a request for factual information, but an angry accusation of guilt. People resent being found guilty without a trial, and they resent your standing in judgment upon them without your ever having been elevated to the bench.

A better technique would be to stop talking about the other person, which is called a "you message," as in, "You make me sick," and choose to use an "I message" instead, such as, "*I am angry at you*" or "*It makes me angry when you pour gravy in my shoes.*" Now the ball is in the other party's court. Let's see what he or she does with it. In the meantime, you are generating less anger in other people and affording yourself some relief from your excessive anger that you were not getting the old way.

People who don't respect themselves are liable to use these inappropriate voices from their childhood. People who have worked through their childhood carryovers are more likely to use a voice that is appropriate to the situation in the present. They can sound firm or gentle, angry or kind. The music changes, but their self-respect stays the same.

#11. CONFRONTATION

To most people, the thought of an anger confrontation is scary. They feel inadequately prepared to cope with anger problems. To prevent this humiliating exposure of their inadequacy, they withdraw from the problem into silence and submission. Their suppressed anger ferments into clinical symptoms such as depression, anxiety and suicidal impulses, or into physical symptoms such as stress, burnout, ulcers, colitis and hypertension. Mismanaged confrontations escalate into domestic violence, drive-by shootings, police brutality, mob demonstrations and even war.

We need not fear that a confrontation will turn into a "shootout at the OK corral." A shouting match need not bring up fears of losing control or being victimized. A confrontation, if it is managed properly, very often clears the air and enables us to get on with the business of living our lives and solving problems.

We are liable to mismanage confrontations because of our vulnerability to taking the other person's anger at us personally, as a wipeout of our self-respect. Under these circumstances, the risks are too high. It isn't worth the risk of losing our self-respect. We submit too soon or we go into an overcompensatory counter-offensive. We lose either way.

It takes courage to solve these problems and that is what we do not have. We do not even know what courage is nor how to attain it. We define courage as the willingness to take a risk. If there were no risk, there would be no need for courage. Without courage, we cannot grow out of our childhood fears and inadequacies. We cannot solve problems without courage. We can only stagnate and fall behind those who are willing to take life as it comes and do the best they can with it. Self-respecting people have courage. They are scared too, but they are willing to take the risk.

The prerequisite for a successful anger exchange is self-respect. This in turn, is the prerequisite for mutual respect. Self-respecting people have the courage to tell the truth, even when that truth is "displeasing." They can speak their unpleasant truths in a mature, responsible manner, such as:

"It makes me angry when you do that."

"I'm glad you can tell me that, because if you don't tell me, I won't know. I'm not a mind reader."

"Are you going to change it?"

"No. It's too late to change it now. It has to be done this way. I don't blame you for being angry, but I'm glad you could tell me. That took courage."

"Can we do it the other way next time?"

"If we prepare for it in the right way, we can give it a try."

The issue is not so much the topic under discussion. It is the positive context in which this conversation takes place. When one person has self-respect, the other person often follows that example. A context of mutual respect is created. If the context is a negative one based on mutual contempt, there can be no constructive outcome. That is when the drive-by shooting starts.

#12. CONSIDER THE SOURCE

When you are under an anger attack, you are so busy reacting to the provocation that you forget to realistically consider the person who is provoking you. It may be your boss, and you see him as ten feet tall, or it may be your sassy three year old whose newly minted cuss word is a threat to your standing in civilized society. It may be the girl of your dreams or a beefy truck driver on the freeway who has just come within two inches of your rear bumper. You tend to invest these people with various fictitious qualities and attributes, which makes it impossible for you to relieve your anger problem in a constructive, nonfatal way.

You can choose to catch yourself inflating or deflating these parties of the second part and then choose not to. You can choose instead, to consider the source of the provocation. The source is, despite these intimidating auras, halos, horns and tusks, an imperfect human being behaving imperfectly as humans are wont to do from time to time. Put in that perspective, their provocation loses some of the power to blow us through the roof. We are now free to say to ourselves, *"It's only Marvin acting up again."*

"Do we only do what we want?"

Rudolph Dreikurs

#13. CRYING

Crying is a healthy, natural way of releasing strong emotion. The Greeks called it a catharsis. Unfortunately, we have developed attitudes towards crying that interfere with this process. We see crying as a sign of weakness to be rejected and despised. We create a conflict between our natural impulse to cry out our anger, and our exaggerated fear of what the neighbors will think. Some of us will never resolve this conflict.

Crying is behavior, and like any behavior, it can have negative as well as positive purposes. When we use our tears for negative purposes, we are making mischief:

1. We use crying to get attention and pity for our suffering. "If I ever stop crying, how can I get the attention that I need to prove that I still exist?"

2. We use crying to obtain power over others and to make them feel guilty and ashamed so that they will do what we want, such as to stop hurting us or take us to the movies. There are more mature techniques for securing cooperation. This misuse of our tears is called "water power."

3. We use our tears to get revenge and to hurt people as they have hurt us. We are reproaching them and punishing them for what they have done. Unfortunately, the issues involved in the negative transaction have not been dealt with constructively and the whole scenario will be repeated shortly.

4. We use tears as an excuse to withdraw from the situation or from our relationships. We lack the courage to find out what is really going on so that the underlying problems can be solved.

When we are depressed -- anger at ourselves in a context of self-contempt -- we cry at the slightest provocation. The issue is not tears; the issue is the unresolved anger that has never been worked through and relieved. After we have sorted out our anger, identified the objects of our anger, peeled our anger artichoke using focusing questions and written our anger letters, the depression lifts and the crying often stops.

Sometimes we weep tears of impotent rage, while other times we weep tears of despair. These tears are legitimate and valid. We need to cry them out on our own terms and not suppress them because of our image. What kind of people cry sometimes? Imperfect human beings cry from time to time and we are worthwhile in spite of it.

#14. DENIAL

A very common method that people have of coping with anger is to deny that they have it: "I am not angry. Shut up." This denial is their way of solving a problem that "nice" or "strong" people are not supposed to have.

We should not make the mistake of penetrating the denial by saying, "Yes, you are angry. Don't lie to me." This makes us sound like an accuser, an attacker or a victimizer, which is exactly what our anger-denying loved ones do not need right now.

They need a friend -- someone who will validate them as a worthwhile human being in spite of the present unpleasantness. We can validate them by validating their anger, which they have just denied having. When they say, "I'm not angry, I'm just hurt," we know that their anger is the emotional response to the hurt. It is down there, but we are not supposed to know it because it is not "nice." We can say something supportive, such as, *"I'd be angry if that happened to me"* or *"The same thing happened to me in fifth grade and I was so angry."* We are giving them permission to follow our example of anger management if they choose to do so.

It is all right if they choose not to. It is their preference right now. Their preference may change in ten minutes. We can wait.

We can even ask a focusing question: *"How do you feel towards people who hurt you?"* The answer that comes out is often "angry."

We do not demand that they confess their anger to us instantly. That is a good intention, but it will backfire. A good intention is our attempt to solve a problem when we really don't know what to do. In order to conceal our feelings of inadequacy to cope, we make up something that sounds good at the time. Our behavior is not reality oriented. It is self-serving and counter-productive. In fact, it is mischief.

We need to have real intentions and to do what reality requires us to do, not what we hope will help but never has in the past. We can say, *"I'm sorry you're so upset. If you would like to talk to me about it later, I'll be glad to listen. If not, that is all right, too."* That is empowering, and it gives them the power of choice when they need it most. They are feeling angry and powerless to do anything about it. *They feel frustrated.* Now they have the power to choose when and if they want to talk to us about their feelings. By giving them a choice, we avoid a power struggle over who can force whom to express what. When we validate the legitimacy of their anger there is nothing for them to deny or rebel against.

If they choose not to talk about it, that is their legitimate preference. We are not going to deny them that preference. It may be their way of testing us to see if we really mean it when we say that we will respect their right to be left alone. Do not flunk the test. They are worthwhile human beings whether they confess their anger or not, and so are you. Sometimes it is appropriate to just let it go and let them heal themselves as best they can. You have already set an example of acceptance and it will help, whether they admit it or not.

#15. DEFENSIVENESS

When people are angry at us, we hear their anger as if it were an attack on our personhood and an assault on our personal worth. This mistake is called "taking it personally." We take their anger personally because we did not know we were not supposed to. Moreover, we do not know how else to take it.

We rise to the defense of our integrity, innocence and high moral character. We cannot see what is wrong with this response. It seems logical to us to meet an attack with a counterattack. This technique never solves the problem.

Our mindless reaction is not logical. The issue is not our character or our worth as a person, the issue is their anger and we need to deal with it effectively and constructively. We cannot do that by saying, "I didn't do it. You lie, I was out of town the whole time."

After we learn that the issue is not one of guilt or innocence, we can let go of our defensive propensities and instead, we can choose to intervene appropriately. Once we have done so, we are free to say, *"I'm sorry that you are so angry,"* or *"It makes you angry when that happens, doesn't it?"* When they hear us empathizing with their pain, they just may calm down so that we can discuss their grievance like equal members of the human race.

#16. DISCRETION

For many years, "total honesty" was a buzzword in the counseling industry. Every self-help book took pride in espousing the high ideal of open honesty at all times. Today, practitioners are reporting that relationships have broken down because of too much honesty. What are we to do?

"Don't just do something, stand there."

Buddha

The first thing that we can do is to stop treating honesty as if it were an isolated attribute that exists apart from our personal context. If our personal context is negative, we are going to have honesty problems. We will have too much or too little. Self-respecting people have fewer honesty problems because they can be appropriately honest.

Appropriate honesty does not mean spilling the beans at every opportunity, nor does it mean telling people the awful truth "for their own good." That is a self-serving good intention. It is an overcompensation for feelings of inferiority by being super-truthful. Our attitude is, "Look how honest I am, everybody. I'm not inferior at all; I'm really superior. I have the power to inflict the truth upon you and you can't stop me."

Discretion does not mean "clamming" up either. We cannot prevent disaster in the future by suppressing unpleasant communication in the present. It takes courage to tell the truth in a discreet manner, as in *"Pardon me, but your spouse has fallen asleep in the punchbowl again."* It takes no courage to look the other way and pretend that it isn't happening.

Self-respecting people do not play these destructive games. They have attributes that immature people do not have -- they have mature judgment and the power of choice. They know how much honesty is appropriate for each given situation. This knowledge enables them to be discreet, which means that they have the ability to decide how much or how little they wish to reveal about themselves. They are not compelled to flaunt their knowledge for overcompensatory purposes. Neither do they suppress information for fear of what others might think. They have the courage to live on their own valid terms.

Sometimes it is appropriate to express our anger openly, other times it is not. Self-respecting people know the difference. When restraint is appropriate, they do not suppress their anger behind a smiling facade and deny that they are angry. They are consciously choosing not to reveal their anger at the present time for legitimate reasons of their own. They may choose to express their anger later, after all the company has gone home, or they may choose to "give it a pass," "consider the source" or write an anger letter. They can choose to mail the letter or to tear it up. That is discretion.

Do's and Don'ts

Do not let other people control your power of choice. If they insist that you be open and honest "for your own good," identify their request as mischief. It does not need to be done. Rather, it is a self-serving good intention on their part. You can choose to say, *"I know you want the best for me and I appreciate it, but I'll be just fine this way,"* or *"Thanks for asking, but I would rather not."* As a worthwhile human being, you have the right to your own preferences.

When someone tries to penetrate or overcome your discretion, do not get into a power struggle over who can make whom tell what. You can choose to deflect the attention away from yourself. You can use focusing questions to expose the underlying purposes of this mischief:

"I wonder why you want to know that."

"In the past, you have used these things as ammunition against me. Are you planning to do that again?"

"Could it be that you are trying to control me? I am not trying to control you. I am only trying to secure your cooperation."

Do not try to make people understand you. Your life goes on whether they understand your motivation or not. You can be discreet about your purposes. They are no one's business but your own.

You can choose to be discreet about your opinions. When someone says, "Your uncle is a lazy bum," you can catch yourself about to play into this mischief. You can choose not to defend or explain. Instead, you can choose to agree that the other person feels that way. You can say, *"You may be right."* You can't fight that. You are setting appropriate limits on the mischief. You are aware that the issue is not your uncle, but power and control. The other person is seeking the power to provoke you into a counterreaction. As a self-respecting person, you are free to make other arrangements.

#17. DISENGAGE FROM THE MISCHIEF

People make mischief at our expense -- they tease, insult, criticize and patronize us. It all makes us angry. The angrier we get, the more they do it. They can't stop and neither can we.

If we want to break this cycle of provocation and anger, we have to figure out what is going on.

Our first step is to identify their provocative behavior as mischief. Mischief is that which does not need to be done. Teasing and criticizing do not need to be done, but they do it anyway. They do it because they can. We don't know how to stop them, so why should they stop when they are winning? We are so easy.

Our second step is to take away from them the power to provoke us with their nonsense. Identifying it as nonsense in the first place helps take some of the impact away from it.

There are two mistakes that we often make when people make mischief. These mistakes make us vulnerable to overreacting to their childish behavior, which always makes things worse.

1. We take their mischief seriously as if it made sense. When they say, *"Can't you do anything right,"* they know very well that we do many things right. That is not the issue. We do

not argue with them or defend our track record. Our track record is not the issue. The issue is that the other person is angry and we need to deal effectively with the anger. We cannot do that if we have made the mistake of taking this exaggerated accusation literally as if it meant what it seems to mean. It just means "I'm angry at what happened just now," and that is what you attend to.

2. We take mischief statements personally, as if they were a reflection on our worth as a person. Our antidote to taking the other person's anger is our self-respect. We can choose to remember that we are a worthwhile human being in spite of our faults and imperfections, one of which seems to have caused them a grievance. We regret that they are angry, but we are not guilty of a crime, nor are we worthless. We are worthwhile in spite of it. Only perfect people can go through life without making their fellow human beings angry, and we are not one of them. We don't have to be.

The third step in the process of disengaging is to respond to the other person's provocation in a way that is appropriate to the situation. For instance, you can say, *"You're right, I'm sorry it happened. I'll take care of it."* If their grievance is not a legitimate one, but only an excuse to get a rise out of us, it is appropriate to return their absurdity with another absurdity. We are now free to say anything we want to say, as long as it is on our terms and not theirs. We can say, *"Isn't it awful? It's been like that all day."* In so saying, we are letting the other person know that they have lost the power to provoke us to madness with their nonsense. They won't stop until we do.

#18. DISENGAGE FROM YOUR OWN GOOD INTENTIONS

Why do we fight with someone we love? It makes no sense on a rational level. No one has ever said after a fight, "You know, I never thought of it that way, mother dear. I see the light. I will change my ways forthwith." But we keep hoping. We keep wanting the best for our loved ones without ever knowing how to bring that about. We never find out how to do that without insulting their intelligence.

On a deeper level, we fight because we have an agenda of our own that has nothing to do with wearing galoshes or eating more roughage. We may, in our hearts, want to "improve" our loved ones so that they will be as happy, prosperous and successful as the law allows. But underneath, we are trying to prove to them how good we are to them. This is how we overcompensate for our feelings that we are really not good enough. Conversely, we may be fighting off the intrusive manipulations of our parents, elder sibling or maiden aunt in order to protect and defend our right to be miserable in our own way. This is a good intention that we have for ourselves. Both parties are engaged in an absurd, mutually destructive struggle over who can make whom happy whose way.

After forty years of trying to change someone in ways that are obviously not working very well, we can choose to stop. We can let go of our ambition to improve people according to our own nebulous specifications. We can let go of our futile efforts to stop them from inflicting their maddening concern up our nose. That is another self-serving good intention. We can disengage ourselves from them. Physically, we can minimize our contacts with them and see if the pattern changes. If it does, we can resume our relationship on a new, more mature basis. However, if the other party is too far gone, we can make the sad decision that the relationship is too painful and destructive for both of us and that it has become necessary to make other arrangements altogether. We can choose not to send good years after bad.

#19. DISPLACEMENT

This is the most common anger mismanagement technique of all. When daddy is angry at his boss, for instance, he cannot very well express his anger directly. He lives in fear of the consequences of his anger -- fear of displeasing, of being victimized, of losing control and of abandonment. He suppresses his anger until he gets home where there is a whole houseful of safe targets. He takes his anger out on his loved ones. They have to take it. He is not powerless anymore. He has power and control over their pain, and the victim has become the victimizer. His problem has been solved at the expense of his loved ones. He cannot see what is wrong with that. He does not see what they have to complain about.

Many of the cases of spouse battering and child abuse that we read about today can be understood as the effects of displaced anger. The original anger may be a few hours old or it may be decades old. The father is displacing his anger at his parents onto his child. The mother may be displacing her anger at her pretty sister onto her pretty daughter. These behaviors are inappropriate, destructive and out of conscious control. They have less to do with current reality than they do with the carryover anger that the individual brings to reality.

Displacers are trying to accomplish three underlying purposes:

1. Relief from the pain of their suppressed rage.

2. Relief from the pain of playing the role of the out of control victim.

3. Revenge upon those who hurt them by hurting others who cannot hurt back.

When these people feel victimized, a dynamic tension is set up and:

1. They feel inferior to their victimizer.

2. This state of inequality is painful and they feel impelled to relieve the pain of their inferiority and worthlessness.

3. They seek this relief by displacing their anger onto others.

4. They build themselves up by tearing others down.

Their equilibrium is restored, while others have just begun to suffer. When these "victims" are able, they will, in turn, seek relief from their torment by following their tormentor's pattern of displacing anger onto safe targets who do not deserve it.

The displacer's cover story is that it is fair to hurt others as they have been hurt. It comes out even. This is not fairness at all, but mischief -- it does not need to be done.

Displacers can feel victimized by another person, by the "system" by life. They may even feel victimized by themselves and think, "Why was I so stupid? The grievance that caused the anger may be real or imaginary, rational or nonrational, but it is a grievance just the same. The pain of it must be assuaged one way or another.

One reason that the father displaces his anger onto his child is that he does not know what else to do. He is following his father's example of problem solving, or perhaps he developed this technique himself on the schoolyard in the third grade. Our antidote is to reveal to him that he has a choice now. He can choose to express his anger verbally like a grown-up or, he can tell his loved ones what the boss said to him at lunch. That will give them the opportunity to validate his anger and give him some relief. But the father cannot do that yet, because showing his feelings would be a sign of "weakness." To overcompensate for this threat of exposure as a "weak," "feeling" person, he demonstrates his awesome power over terrified women and children. This is not strength, but phony, overcompensatory "strongness." It is an absurd attitude. He does not respect himself on an appropriate basis and he will not stop beating up his loved ones until he does.

We can encourage him to make this new choice on his own behalf by asking, *"Did something happen to make you angry?"* This question shows that we respect him in spite of his emotional imperfection. No one ever showed him respect under these circumstances before. In time, he may come to respect himself. It will be easier for him to express his real feelings. That will take courage. That will take strength.

#20. DO THE UNEXPECTED

When you are angry, you are very vulnerable to being manipulated to your own detriment. Your usually acute thought processes have been swamped by a tide of nonrational reactions and counterreactions. You are, in this state, very likely to do exactly what your sparring partners expect you to do. They do not expect you to do anything reasonable or constructive. They expect you to be as immature and vindictive as they are. "That's fair." You accommodate them when you sink down to their nonsensical level of discourse. "You stink." *"I do not stink."* "Yes you do." *"You take that back."*

You will get nowhere that way. One of you has to make a break for it. If they do not know how, then you must. You know by now, after the two hundredth time, exactly what they expect you to do when they provoke you. You can choose, when you are ready, not to do it. You can choose to do something else instead. In fact, you can do anything you want to as long as it is on your own terms and not a mindless reaction to their provocation. If you are tired of this useless third-grade game, you can learn some new responses to old jabs:

"Self-respecting people are not driven to succeed, they are free to succeed."

Rudolph Dreikurs

More Game-Enders

They say:	They do not expect you to say:
"You stink."	*"There's a lot of it going around."*
"You're stupid, too."	*"I don't know how you stand it."*
"This report isn't as good as Miss Rumplemeyer used to turn out, bless her soul."	*"Yes, she was a saint, wasn't she. Too bad she died so young."*
"Come back here and fight like a man."	*"Second graders fight. Grown-ups do not. I am leaving now. I hope you feel better in the morning."*
"I hate you."	*"I am sorry you are so angry."*
"I am not angry. That's stupid."	*"You could have fooled me."*

As you can see, the content of your reply does not have to make sense. You are using your response to reveal to your partner that the game is over and that you have ended it. You have done what reality has required you to do.

They can no longer control you into reacting on their terms. You have a choice now, an alternative mode of responding. This alternative gives you a 100 percent improvement over the old days when you had only one choice, a knee-jerk reaction to defend yourself, which was not much of a selection to choose from.

#21. DO YOUR HOMEWORK

In our vignettes, we show people doing their homework. This is an important concept in our system of anger management. A homework is an action that we take on our own behalf. It is not against the other person -- it is for us. We are not reacting to a provocation, but are taking an independent, appropriate action that the reality of the situation requires us to take. We have used our adult judgment to sort out what reality does and does not require and we have made a decision based on that judgment. We must now have the courage to do what we have decided to do. When we accomplish this task, we have done our homework.

The payoff for doing our homework is the ensuing feeling of accomplishment, success and confidence that we can do it again. Identity, maturity, trust in our judgment, security within ourselves, liberation from our childhood fears and doubts, feelings of equality, belonging, appropriate responsibility and competence are our rewards. We will also experience relief from our tension, pressure and stress -- we will feel peace of mind.

These feelings are all components of self-respect. Each time we do our homework, especially an anger homework, we take another step towards outgrowing our childhood roles and replacing them with a mature identity in the present. We are using these negative situations as opportunities to grow. We are replacing our self-contempt with self-respect.

Until we do our homework, all of this is theoretical and hypothetical. After we have done our homework, it is not theoretical anymore and we can feel it. We have been there and we made it happen. We feel in control, not of the other person or the relationship, but of ourselves. We have earned the right to respect

ourselves as worthwhile human beings in spite of our faults and imperfections.

#22. DON'T GET MAD, GET EVEN

This is a new name for an old mischief called revenge. It is as old as Cain and Abel. It has made all of the wars in history longer and bloodier than they would have been otherwise. It is the energy that erupts in shootouts on our freeways, sidewalks and bedrooms. There is nothing cute about it.

First of all, it is too late to say, "don't get mad." You are already mad or you wouldn't be thinking about getting even. You are denying your anger and you will pay the price for your foolishness.

Secondly, getting even with your provoker does not constitute "problem solving," even though some folks thought it did. At least they thought so when they were alive.

Thirdly, your getting even with them entitles them, under the "fair trade laws" to get even with you. There are places in the world this very day where the residents have been getting even with each other for hundreds of years. It is not a pretty sight.

Civilized human beings do not seek revenge. It is mischief that does not need to be done. They do not go for counterrevenge, either. They resolve their anger problems in ways that integrate their head and their heart, which takes a little more forethought. It is not nearly as exciting, but they do not mind.

#23. DON'T LET THEM MAKE YOU ANGRY

This technique is a product of American psychology, which holds that, "The issue is the issue, and if you don't like it, get rid of it." American psychology advocates such techniques as "will power," "pulling yourself up by your bootstraps" and "self-motivation." It also recommends "putting the past behind you. It's dead, forget about it." The goal is to have a nation of perfectly nice people acting perfectly nice to each other at all times. "Play nice and don't fight," seems to be one of its watchwords.

Their line on anger management seems to be, "No one can make you angry unless you let them, so don't let them." The implication is that if you become angry, it is your own fault for being weak and not strong. It is not your advisor's fault that his techniques did not work. That is your fault, too.

We are seeing in these pages that the *real* issue is what you bring to the present grievance from your childhood. You have unresolved issues from the past that are ignited by analogous situations in the present. It is not a weakness in your character when this happens, it is human nature. It is one of your many faults and imperfections. You are worthwhile in spite of it. Blaming the individual for having human imperfections is not an encouraging technique.

With the right kind of help, you can have insight into your private agenda of childhood carryovers that predispose you to overreact in the present. The past is not dead and gone. It is alive in you right now, and, to some extent, it is interfering with your relationships.

The issue is not "letting" them make you angry in the sense of failing to prevent this incoming provocation. You are not made of stone, and you are not required to be.

When your open wounds from the past are cleaned in the right way and allowed to heal properly, you will be less vulnerable to the provocative mischief of the people around you. There will not be as much anger to manage as there is now, and you will be able to manage it much better than you have ever managed it before. You will never be able to manage it perfectly, but you are not required to do that, either.

Example isn't the best way to teach self-respect, it's the only way. "

Albert Schweitzer

"Man is the only animal that never fully matures."

Rudolph Dreikurs

#24. DON'T TAKE IT PERSONALLY

Our biggest vulnerability to an anger attack is our susceptibility to taking things personally. When something makes us angry, for instance, our ten year old is called out at first by the Little League umpire, we become angry at the "wrongness" and the "unfairness" of it all. We are angry at our powerlessness to do anything about it. These are all facets of our anger attack, and they are painful. But the biggest pain comes when we take our child's grievance personally, as if it were a reflection on our worth as a person. Then our anger turns to super-anger. We lose control, we overreact and do something irrational that we will be sorry for.

Anger management means identifying these predispositions that we acquired in childhood and learning how to replace them with more appropriate predispositions in the present. In this case, we can catch ourselves taking these ups and downs of everyday life personally and choose not to. Instead, we can replace our feelings of self-doubt with feelings of self-respect. *"I am a worthwhile human being whether my kid is tagged out at first or not. My kid is a worthwhile human being, too."* We can also say, *"I am a worthwhile human being whether my boss shakes my hand or not. My worth is not dependent upon these external considerations. I am a worthwhile human being in spite of my faults and imperfections. That is my antidote to taking things more personally than I need to take them."*

#25. DRAW A PICTURE

Children have much to be angry about, but they have trouble expressing their anger. Some of them have never learned the proper names for their feelings, while others have learned not to express feelings for fear of being beaten. They also have feelings about their feelings such as "feelings are bad," which makes their problems too complicated to articulate clearly. So they keep their feelings in to be on the safe side. Children cannot control much, but they have learned to "control" their feelings if they know what is good for them.

We want to encourage them to let their feelings out in the right way so that they can get the relief they need right now, not twenty years from now in a therapist's office.

If they cannot use a verbal medium, we can try another. We can give them paper and coloring materials and suggest that they draw their anger. We do not structure it too much for them, for it has to be their expression.

Afterwards we do not say, "That's a beautiful picture." We say, *"That's very interesting. Tell me about it."* We focus on their anger. *"What angered you the most when that happened? Who are you angry at? Who else are you angry at?"* Very often they are angry at themselves for failing to prevent the grievance. This is the anger that tears down their self-respect.

We can also say, *"If this person could talk, what would they say?"* and *"What would this other person say?"* If they want to stab the paper or tear it up, we must let them. That is part of the process. The child is more important than the piece of paper. If the child needs to draw another picture tomorrow, that is all right, too.

When we see that the child has had some relief from the pent-up emotion, we can ask, *"How did you feel after you drew your picture?"* We can run down the facets of self-respect that we think are appropriate for the child's age. *"Did you feel relief? Did you feel that you were making this picture happen? That is control. Did you feel a sense of accomplishment and success? Can you do it again? That is confidence. Did you feel like you belonged? Well, you do. You belong to yourself and to the whole human race."*

DRAW A PICTURE

Do's and Don'ts

Do not have good intentions for these children, let them have real intentions for themselves.

Do not worry about the mess. Messes can be cleaned up. Neatness does not count.

Do not defend the people they are angry at. They are not the issue. The issue is the children's anger.

Do not try to make a child "understand." That is intellectualizing and it defeats the purpose.

When you validate children's anger, you validate them as worthwhile human beings in spite of this unpleasantness. You also validate yourself. That is emotional first aid.

#26. EMOTIONAL FIRST AID

In your first aid manual, the first thing it tells you to do is to stop the bleeding. Wouldn't it be nice if there were a way of putting a tourniquet on a loved one or a co-worker who was raging out of control or silently bleeding inside from a grievous hurt.

Well, there is. First, you have to find the "bleeding" or the anger, which is not as easy as it sounds. Your teenage son may use words like "upset," "hate" or "I don't like it" to describe the situation that tore him apart. These are euphemisms for anger. He may even deny that he is angry at all and attack you for suggesting that he is. "I am not angry. Shut up!"

It is like a drowning victim who is beating off the lifeguard who is trying to save him. The professional lifeguard does not say, "Ok, fella, if that's the way you're going to be, go ahead and drown. See if I care." You persevere and are not put off by these inappropriate behaviors and mischief that arise under emotional stress. You disengage emotionally from their mischief. You even disengage from your own mischief. You do not say, "That's the thanks I get for trying to be helpful. Well, I won't make that mistake again." After you have disengaged, you are free to address the real issues behind the smokescreen that they have thrown up. The issue is not "hate," it is anger.

After you have identified their emotion properly as anger, you proceed to call their anger by its rightful name. You say something like, *"I'm sorry you are so angry"* or *"What happened to make you so angry?"* Calling their anger to their attention in this way gives them a handle on what is going on inside of them, a gearshift that they can use to manage their out of control feelings. It is up to them to use this tool constructively, but they cannot use it if someone does not put it into their hands. Very often, this alone will stop the bleeding. You have validated their anger as a legitimate, though unpleasant emotion, and you have validated them as worthwhile in spite of it. If you do it right, you will even find that you have validated yourself.

#27. EUPHEMIZING

This technique involves the solving of anger problems by calling them something else, "I'm not angry. I'm just miffed, tiffed and spiffed." By so saying, these angry people are able to deny to themselves and others that they have a "not nice" emotion in their bosom. The purpose of their denial is to prevent the negative consequences that they are sure would follow if they were to utter the "A" word, such as rejection, victimization, loss of control, loss of love, loss of prestige, disapproval and being sent to their room.

These deniers are also preventing the painful feelings of guilt that "nice" people feel when they fail to be perfectly pleasing. To them, these griefs are not worth the trouble of calling their anger by its legal name, so they trivialize their own emotion. By extension, they are also trivializing themselves. Moreover, they are keeping themselves from getting the relief that they might get if they were to acknowledge the legitimacy and validity of this unsettling but unavoidable aspect of their earthly existence.

These cutesy names for anger, which include "ballistic," "bummed out," "bent out of shape" and so on, can be called "downscale" euphemisms. There are also "upscale" terminologies such as "hostility," "outrage," "violence," "acting out," "passion," "aggressiveness," etc. These words are often used to enhance the impressiveness and potency of our homely, garden variety anger. These euphemisms, too, make the anger problem worse instead of better. We are putting on airs in order to distance ourselves from the earthy emotion that we feel in our hearts. This is another example of overcompensation for feelings of inferiority.

Sometimes we use euphemisms because we think daddy really is "grumpy," "grouchy," "mean," "in a bad mood," "crabby," "hateful," "cranky," "down" and a hundred other stand-ins for the offensive sounding but, more definitive word, "angry."

#28. FAMILY-FREE DIET

If chocolate makes us break out in a rash, we make the sad decision to put ourselves on a chocolate-free diet for our own good. By the same token, if we see that our family reunions do nothing but upset us for weeks afterwards, we may have to make other arrangements.

Our families have come to see us in a certain role since we were five years old. Our loved ones will not let us outgrow our childhood role as "The Victim," "The Stupid Child" or "The Loser." No matter how competent we are in the outside world, they treat us the same way they did when we were a clumsy kindergartner. The more we yell at them to start treating us like a grown-up, the more we confirm that they are correct in their assessment of our mental state. It is maddening.

"Power is an issue only when it is contested."

Rudolph Dreikurs

One way to manage our anger at these obtuse folks is to stay away from them. It may be sad and lonely, but they may come to respect us at last. It will be the smartest thing we have done in twenty years. They may have been wondering how long it would take us to catch on.

After we have been on our family-free diet for a while, we can test the waters. We can call or go over there to see if anything has changed. They may have missed us during the interim, maybe even learned to appreciate our good qualities. Maybe nothing has changed. Either way, we do not have much to lose by staying away, except hours and hours of abuse and grief that they do not need any more than you do.

#29. FIGHTING

Some of us mismanage our anger by fighting. We see physical aggression as an outlet for our pent-up energies. It is an outlet all right, but at what price? When two people have been raised by parents who were evenly matched fighters, they are compatible with this "problem-solving" technique. However, when one of the parties has been raised in a fight-free environment, it is a different matter. This is called a "mixed marriage." The husband may feel comfortable having a good, clean fight like his parents. In his view, this is how loving couples solve problems. There are no hard feelings afterward, they kiss and make up. Sometimes they cannot kiss *unless* there has been a fight. The nonfighting wife, however, sees confrontation as barbaric and scary. It is foreign to her upbringing. She refuses to participate. The husband feels "betrayed" by her refusal to "cooperate" with him. His expectation of emotional release is thwarted. They begin to fight over fighting.

When does a disagreement turn into a fight? When one of the parties takes an issue personally. As soon as that happens, the original issue is no longer the issue. The issue has now become the individual's self-respect. The other party is often not aware that this subtle shift has taken place. These two are now arguing on two different wavelengths and there cannot be a rational resolution of their differences.

Our hope in writing this book is that you will be enabled to fight smarter, not harder. We hope, for instance, that you will respect yourself on a new basis so that a difference of opinion will not cost you your self-respect. We also hope that you will be able to identify the mischief component in the dispute. *"This does not need to be done. I can choose to disengage from it and resume the conversation at a more appropriate time and place."* You can identify the anger component in the argument and when it is reaching dangerous levels, you can use your new-found power of choice to make other arrangements.

We hope that you are learning a new and better definition of control. Control does not mean preventing bad things from happening. People resent being controlled for their own good because it implies that they are stupid and inadequate. A fight often starts over who can inflict whose good intentions upon whom.

Most fights are over absurdities. The precipitating factor is often trivial, such as burnt toast. If one partner sees burnt toast as a reminder of irresponsibility from the past or a victimization by a loved one, then all bets are off and the fight is on.

We can no longer afford this horrendous loss of time, energy and love. We cannot afford to keep destroying our potential for happiness in these mindless squabbles over absurdities. Life is too short to spend it wrangling over Aunt Blanche's thoughtless remark. We can "Consider the Source," "Give It a Pass" or any other of the many anger management techniques in this book. We will be giving emotional first aid to ourselves, to our partner and to our relationship. When we learn to fight smarter, we may find that we do not have to fight at all.

"Mischief is that which does not need to be done."

Rudolph Dreikurs

Four Steps to Fighting Smarter

1. Identify the problem. What is the real issue behind the surface issue? Ask a focusing question:

    "What happened to make you so angry?"
    "What angered you the most?"

    For example, the other person might say, "I was trying to help and you wouldn't let me." *"Could it be that you had good intentions for me?"* "That's right, I meant well and you didn't appreciate it." *"Could it be that you feel that your 'goodness' was all for nothing?"* "I sure do." *"I'm sorry that you are so angry at me for not appreciating you, but who else are you angry at besides me?"* "I'm angry at myself for trying too hard to be helpful. Maybe I should stop trying so hard." *"Maybe I would appreciate you more if you did."*

2. Neither fight nor give in. Fighting is negative cooperation and it takes two. If one of you stops, the fight becomes irrelevant. As soon as you fight, you lose. You can choose to disengage from the fight, which is only mischief, at any time.

3. Secure positive cooperation. You can choose to replace your negative cooperation with positive cooperation. You can ask, *"What remedy do you seek?"*

4. Establish an atmosphere of mutual respect:

    a) You must respect yourself.
    b) You must respect the other person.
    c) The other person must respect you.
    d) The other person must respect himself.

    This atmosphere of mutual respect is hard to establish, but fighting is even harder.

5. Do what you can do. You can catch yourself depending on the other person to solve the problem. You have left yourself out of the equation. You have the power of choice and adult competencies. There are many things that you cannot do, but you *can* use your adult judgment to tell you what you can do instead. It is then your responsibility to do it on your own valid terms. When you do, you will be replacing your dependency with independence.

#30. FIND THE PURPOSE

We understand human behavior not in terms of such causes as peer pressure, television violence, socioeconomic deprivation, breakdown of the family or low self-esteem, but in terms of its purposes. When you misbehave, you may not be consciously aware of your purposes, but you have them just the same. You acquired your attitudes and purposes early in life and you have not examined them since the day you acquired them. You are not a mindless rat in a maze, but a member of the human race. Laboratory rats do not have purposes, they have drives. Human beings have purposes.

For example, your tardiness makes people angry and their anger makes you angry. You do not need this warfare, but you keep coming late anyway. You might ask yourself a focusing question. Not, "Why am I doing this?" It is not that easy. Your psyche will defend itself against exposing your infantile, potentially humiliating foibles even to you. It will come up with something useless such as, "I try so hard to be on time. I guess I'm just built that way. I can't help it." As an adult now, you can go about getting the answer in a more productive way. You can ask yourself a focusing question, *"How would my life be different if I stopped coming late?"* Here are some of the answers that you may get:

1. "I'd be happy." The purpose of your tardiness may be to keep you from getting any happiness that you believe you do not "deserve."

2. "I wouldn't be rebelling against my father anymore." Perhaps you are trying to prove your independence from your father by disobeying his order to come on time. He isn't even around anymore. This is not adult independence, it is only rebellious mischief.

3. "If I screw up the little things, I won't have to cope with the big things in life. I know I'd fail if I tried. By coming late, I prevent myself from failing at the larger tasks. It is the lesser misery that I prefer to the greater misery of failing across the board."

4. "They might not notice me if I came at the same time as everyone else, and if people do not notice me, how can I be sure I exist?"

5. "If I get there early, other people will have the power to keep me waiting. I will feel powerless and out of control. I'd rather keep them waiting for me. That way I am in control."

6. "I am angry at these people, but I dare not express my anger openly. I can punish them by keeping them waiting. Why should I stop? It's working."

7. "I'd be seen as a responsible person but I was never the responsible person in my family growing up. My sister Suzie was the responsible one. I'm just the baby of the family, always bringing up the rear. At least I'm consistent."

These are all negative purposes that underly our mischief. Self-respecting people can identify these qualities in themselves and replace them with more positive purposes in their lives. The more self-respecting we are, the more positive and constructive our purposes will be and the more likely we will be to come on time.

Negative Purposes

Our underlying purpose usually turns out to be to prevent something bad from happening, like "losing control," "failing," "feeling guilty," being exposed and humiliated or ceasing to exist. Our goal sounds positive, but upon further examination, its negativity becomes apparent. "Preventing" is a negative approach to solving problems, and predicting a negative outcome that has to be prevented is an exercise in pessimistic fortune-telling. We are setting ourselves up to fail because we cannot do it. We are not fortune-tellers. When we hear ourselves saying, "What's the use, I am going to fail anyway," this is not ESP, but our discouragement and self-doubt talking to us. Self-doubt cannot be optimistic and happy. It can only be negative and counter-productive.

Self-Talk - The Antidote to Negative Purposes

Old Tapes	New Tapes
1. "My negative purpose, now that I have identified it, is in the service of my feelings of inadequacy and worthlessness."	*"When I remember that I am a worthwhile human being in spite of my faults and imperfections, my negative purposes will become irrelevant."*
2. "My purpose is to prevent happiness, which to you is a positive quality, but to me is a negative quality. I'm afraid I'll be caught enjoying happiness that I do not deserve to enjoy. I'll feel guilty. It isn't worth it. I have to keep it from happening."	*"Worthless people don't deserve to enjoy happiness, but self-respecting people do. As a worthwhile human being, I can catch myself sabotaging my happiness and stop it."*

Old Tapes	New Tapes
3. "My purpose is to prevent success because I know that I won't be able to keep it up. My inadequacies will catch up to me and my success will end in failure, so why bother succeeding in the first place?"	*"I am not inadequate or incompetent. I only feel that way sometimes. I deserve to succeed and I am competent enough to take life as it comes and do the best I can with it. If I have ups and downs, it will prove merely that I am imperfect. I am worthwhile in spite of it. I am not required to succeed perfectly and forever."*
4. "My purpose is to maintain and perpetuate my unhappy childhood perception of myself. I cling to this role because I do not know what will take its place. Maybe nothing. That is too scary."	*"As a self-respecting adult, I know that my childhood roles will be replaced by a mature identity, and it's about time. I can stop living in the past and stop trying to prevent the future. I can choose to start living in the present."*
5. "My purpose is to prevent losing control. I never knew what control was; I only thought I did. I have been out of control all my life. I must hang on for dear life to keep from going over the cliff."	*"Control means taking life as it comes, not preventing disaster. I couldn't take life as it came when I was a child. I can now. I can choose to stop hanging on to thin air. I can let go of these mistaken attitudes from the past."*

#31. FOCUSING QUESTION

When we are angry, we are up in arms, carried away with our emotions, we are not using our heads. Civilized people have learned to use their heads in the right way, not to suppress their anger or rationalize it away, but to sort out what is real from what is not real.

We can do that by asking ourselves, *"What is angering me the most right now? Is it the fact that I didn't make the sale? No. That is merely the occasion for my anger. What angers me the most is that I am feeling victimized by this customer. I am feeling unappreciated and good for nothing."*

The next focusing question might be, *"Who am I angry at? The customer, of course. Who else am I angry at? I am angry at me for being so 'stupid' and for not doing it the right way. I am taking this whole thing personally and feeling worthless."*

These focusing questions have helped us get at the issues beneath the surface issues. Now we can work through them in a more appropriate, mature perspective:

"I am not a victim. I am an imperfect human being."

"It is not a matter of fairness. It is just business, that's all. I win a few, I lose a few. I am worthwhile in spite of it."

"I am not dependent on my customers or this sale for my personal worth. They cannot make me feel good for nothing -- I am worthwhile in spite of them."

"I am not stupid or worthless. I need not be angry at myself. I did the best I could at the time. I'll try them again next month. I am a self-respecting human being in the meantime" (see #55, Peeling Your Anger Artichoke).

#32. FORGIVING OTHERS

As we have seen, the first step towards managing our anger appropriately is the identification of the mistaken attitudes and convictions that predispose us to being excessively angry in the first place. Once these mistakes have been corrected, we will be less likely to fly off the handle than we were in the past.

The second step is the identification of those factors from our childhood that prevent us from expressing our anger as appropriately as we otherwise might. These factors include fear, denial, parental examples, family constellation, etc. These impediments can be removed so that our suppressed anger will not compound itself inside of us, as it has been doing for years.

The third step is to relieve our residual anger by writing anger letters to those who have caused us grievances in the past.

The fourth step in the process is learning appropriate modes of expressing our legitimate anger so that we can begin to cope effectively with anger-provoking situations as they come up.

But the management of our anger does not end in the instant that we articulate our anger in these new, appropriate ways. There remains one last stage in the process that must be completed in order to bind up the wounds left by this devastating emotion. If we do not complete this "mopping-up" stage, we will carry the festering residue of our rage in our hearts forever.

To Forgive or Not To Forgive

The antidote to our anger is forgiveness. Many of us cannot bring ourselves to forgive those who have "trespassed against us." Below the level of conscious awareness, there are attitudes and predispositions that prevent us from relieving our residual anger in this way, and we carry grudges in our hearts for years. These impediments to forgiveness are carryovers from our childhood, when we learned all kinds of things about ourselves and about life that were not true. They are not true now and they weren't true then, but we behave as if they were. We do not even know that they are there.

One carryover from our childhood is our total ignorance of what "forgiveness" means. In the absence of an appropriate working definition, we make up inappropriate, mistaken definitions. Then, we proceed to withhold forgiveness according to our misdefinition.

We imagine that forgiveness is arrived at through a logical, rational sorting-out process of assessing degrees of guilt and innocence or the relative evil of the perpetrator's intent, as if we were a Supreme Court of one. This mistaken "scientific" approach to relieving our pent-up anger is another example of "rationalitosis," which means trying to solve nonrational problems rationally.

Some of us "forgive" too soon. We say things like, "Oh, they didn't mean to do what they did. They didn't know any better." We would say that reality required these people to find out what they didn't know, but they failed to assume that responsibility. We suffered as a direct consequence of their negligence.

Some of us try to wish away our anger by saying, "They were doing the best they could." Here, we would say that they were not doing their best at all. They were behaving out of their ignorance, discouragement and self-contempt. They caused us a legitimate grievance and it made us angry. We have a right to our anger and we must not sugarcoat it by forgiving our victimizers on these superficial bases. We will never get rid of our anger if we do. This type of "forgiveness" is no more than a "good intention" that we have for our perpetrators. We need to replace these good intentions with real intentions for ourselves.

Forgiveness is not arrived at or achieved intellectually. Our anger is a subjective, nonrational problem and it must be solved subjectively. That means replacing one subjective feeling or emotion with another subjective feeling or emotion. When we are angry, we are, in a sense, at war. We must replace these warlike feelings in our bloodstream with the feeling that we are at peace.

How is that done? Before we can show how that is done, let us identify some of the most common impediments to replacing our angry feelings with feelings of peace, serenity within ourselves and blessed relief from the pressure, stress and tension of lifelong warfare within ourselves.

The Impediments to Forgiveness

These are some of the unconscious attitudes that prevent us from forgiving others:

1. "Why should I forgive them? They never forgive me. It's not fair."

   "How are you helping the cause of justice and fairness by harboring this anger inside of you forever? It doesn't work that way."

2. "When I am angry, there is nothing I can do about it. I feel so powerless and depressed."

   "There is something you can do. There is one power that you have and that is the power to forgive and give yourself some relief."

3. "No one ever told me that I had the power to forgive. I've been so busy asking people to forgive me that I never realized that I had the power to forgive them."

"You are not a child any more. Adults have the power to forgive anyone they want to."

4. "Who am I to forgive anyone? I'm nobody."

"You are not a nobody. You are a worthwhile human being in spite of your faults and imperfections. You have as much right to forgive as anyone else, no more and no less."

5. "Why should I bother to forgive them? They don't care whether or not I forgive them, so what's the use?"

"You are not doing it for them. You are doing it for yourself. This is a choice you can make on your own terms in order to relieve your own pent-up emotions."

6. "Why should I forgive them? What they did was wrong."

"Do we only forgive people who do right? Such people don't need our forgiveness."

7. "I cannot forgive them. It is my moral responsibility to condemn these wretches forever for what they did!"

"Your eternal righteous indignation makes you feel morally superior to these wretches. Big deal, morally superior to a wretch! Your superiority is fiction. You can choose to set a limit on your responsibility for judging the imperfections of your fellow human beings. You are not more human than they are, nor are they less human than you. They are only imperfect human beings, and their imperfections made you angry."

8. "It's the principle of the thing. I must not compromise my abstract ideals even though they have nothing to do with the real world."

"You must catch yourself trying to relieve your painful feeling of inferiority by identifying yourself with high sounding and irrational abstractions such as:

a) 'If my kids make me unhappy, I am entitled to make them unhappy. That's fair!'

b) 'I am their parent and I am entitled to their respect whether I know what I am talking about or not. I don't care if I have to beat it out of them.'

c) 'I am trying to make this a better world by stamping out rudeness, offensiveness, inconsiderateness and other forms of not acting appropriately. If I start forgiving these incorrect people, what will the world come to?'

These are not principles or ideals at all. They are self-serving, overcompensatory attitudes carried over from childhood. Super-angry idealists can relieve themselves of these destructive determinants of their behavior by reminding themselves that they are worthwhile human beings on their own terms, not because they are upholding some absurd good intention from first grade. "

9. "I have been carrying this anger for so long that it's like a harpoon in my side. It is a part of me. I am afraid that if I pull it out, I will bleed to death. I don't know who or what I would be without it. I will be annihilated. It's scary."

"It is true that your old role as the angry, impotent victim will begin to fall away from you after you have

chosen to forgive. But you will not be left in a void. In place of this unhappy role you will find an identity of your own as a worthwhile human being in spite of your faults and imperfections. You will feel better about yourself and about your life than you ever did."

10. "If I forgive them, I might become like one of them and I don't want that to happen."

"Your defense against losing your identity is not your suppressed rage. That is not what sets you apart from the people who hurt you. You are more than a bundle of anger. You are a worthwhile human being in spite of your faults and imperfections."

"Once you have experienced yourself in these new terms, you will not be like anybody else, you will have an independent identity of your own."

11. "If I forgive them, it will be as if I were condoning what they did."

"Do not confuse forgiveness with condoning. Condone means to let pass without punishment. You are not being asked to condone their behavior nor to punish them, but to forgive them for perpetrating it. It is written, 'Hate the sin, not the sinner.' Hating these sinners poisons our lives and does not have much of an effect on them in the end anyway."

12. "Why should I give them the satisfaction of forgiving them?"

"Are you living your life in terms of depriving others of satisfaction? That is a negative ambition and it cannot be a very gratifying lifestyle for you. Moreover, it does not deprive them of anything they can't live

without. It's a game that you are playing with yourself.
You can choose to live your life on more realistic
terms. "

13. "If I forgive them they will keep doing it. I have
    forgiven them three times already and they haven't
    stopped."

    "The purpose of forgiveness is not to control or
    prevent behavior. It is to give you some relief from
    your pain. It may be that you have been forgiving them
    in the wrong way and they are taking advantage of
    your vulnerability. Forgiving them in the right way and
    for the right purposes will make you less vulnerable,
    whether they stop doing it or not. Your good intention
    is to change them for the better so that they will stop
    hurting you. You need to replace this useless good
    intention with a real intention to change yourself. You
    need to do some homework in your own behalf. You
    can choose to set limits on their behavior by leaving
    earlier or by imposing some other logical consequence.
    You will feel stronger in your self-respect after you
    have done so. They will respect you more, too. That is
    when they will stop. "

14. "I am afraid that if I forgive them it will make me
    vulnerable to being hurt again in the future."

    "Where is it written that if you don't forgive, it will
    make you tough and invulnerable? You cannot prevent
    hurtful things from happening to you in the future by
    refusing to forgive. There is no connection between
    unforgiveness and security. As a worthwhile human
    being you can cope with hurtful things in the future as
    they come, just like anyone else. You don't need to
    prevent them from happening. In the meantime, you

can choose to live in the present and do the best you can with it. That is a positive ambition."

15. "If I forgive them, my suffering might stop. I'm not sure that I am worthy to get relief from my suffering. All I have ever deserved is to suffer. It might make me happy. I'm not sure I deserve that. Besides, if I ever stop suffering, what will I have to talk about?"

   "You have suffered long enough. As a worthwhile human being, you deserve to be as happy as anyone else, no more and no less."

16. "If I forgive them, I will forfeit my entitlement to get revenge on them someday."

   "You are afraid that if you forgive them, the judge will throw your case out of court. This is fiction. Does this dream of vindication in the unspecified future make you happy? Or does it merely prevent you from living your life in the meantime? Life is too short for this mean, petty spitefulness. You pay a high price for reserving the right to be as cruel to them as they were to you. Besides, revenge promises a lot more than it delivers."

17. "If I forgive them, I might have to start living my life in the present and assuming appropriate responsibility for my own situation. If I did that, I might fail. It's much safer to hide behind my old grudges and resentments."

   "You are using your ancient grievances as an excuse to withdraw from your appropriate tasks and responsibilities in the present. You are seeking to exempt yourself from having to cope with life because you are afraid you'll fail if you try. But hiding behind your anger is a fictitious solution to a pseudo-problem.

You need not live in fear of failure to assume your responsibilities perfectly or to exempt yourself from tasks that other people seem to be accomplishing without too much difficulty. If you can learn to respect yourself as a worthwhile human being, you will be able to find the courage that it takes to do the best you can with what you've got. If you slip up, it will only prove that you are an imperfect human being. You are worthwhile in spite of it."

18. "If I forgive, I'll forfeit my right to get angry again."

"Forgiveness now does not preclude becoming angry again. You can always forgive again if you do."

19. "My parents never forgave anybody. If I start now, I will betray their ideal of eternal grudge bearing."

"Is there no better way to honor our mothers and fathers than to uphold their mistaken coping techniques? You can honor them by being all you can be, and that means throwing this dead weight overboard and respecting their best, not their worst."

20. "If I forgive them, it means that I have to go over there and kiss them on the cheek. I'd rather die!"

"There is no such 'have to.' Cheek kissing is entirely optional. Do not confuse forgiveness with reconciliation."

Logical Consequences

We are not the impotent victims of these offenders. Neither are we the passive prisoners of our own anger. We have the power of choice now. We can choose to liberate ourselves from these unhappy roles by doing some homework in our own behalf.

One homework that we can do is to impose a logical consequence upon the people who have hurt us. We can choose to outgrow the illogical consequences that we have been using since childhood such as:

Muttering under our breath.

Nursing our anger in our hearts forever.

Calling them dirty names.

Holding our breath until we turn blue.

We did not invent these techniques out of our adult intelligence. They represent childhood solutions to anger problems that we did not know how to solve way back when.

Logical consequences, on the other hand, are the product of our mature judgment and experience. They are appropriate to the reality of the situation as we see it. They are not childish, self- indulgent or irresponsible. They are appropriately responsible choices that we have made in order to relieve the painful pressure that our unresolved anger problem is causing us. Our logical consequence is not a good intention to straighten somebody out. It is not for their good but for our own.

These are some logical consequences that we can use the next time we have an anger problem:

1. We can tell the truth: *"That makes me angry."*

2. We can write an anger letter.

3. We can choose whether or not to mail it.

4. We can deprive the offender of our company for an appropriate length of time, up to and including forever.

5. We can tell the offender about our grievance and what it has cost us emotionally and otherwise. We can let him know what he can do to compensate us for our losses.

6. We can put a frog in his underwear drawer. It isn't logical, but it always gets a laugh. No one can be logical all the time.

What a different world this would be if all the wife beaters, child abusers, politicians, generals, zealots, judges, managers and motorists on the planet would start using logical consequences every day instead of what they have been using all their lives (see #49, Logical Consequences).

What Is Forgiveness?

We have just seen some of the things that forgiveness is not. It is not "condoning," "permitting" or "allowing." It is not for the anger maker's benefit, but for our own. We define forgiveness as a *letting go of anger*. It is a conscious, deliberate choice that we make to stop holding onto our rage or the memory of our rage. We have the power of choice and we can choose to let it go. This does not concern the perpetrator of our grievance at all. He need never know what we have chosen to do in our own behalf. It is none of his business. This is between us and us.

After we have confessed our anger and forgiven our perpetrators, what will take its place in our heart? We will find that our anger, with its consequent tension, pressure, anxiety and stress, has been replaced with feelings of relief; openness to life; liberation (*"I have freed myself from the old roles that I used to play"*); identity (*"I am the one who made the forgiveness happen"*);

living in the present instead of the past and all the other facets of self-respect. We have done our homework on our own behalf. We have assumed appropriate responsibility for our own emotional well-being and we have given ourselves emotional first aid. As a consequence, we will experience ourselves as the experiencer of our lives.

#33. FORGIVING OURSELVES

Forgiving others is difficult, but it is even more difficult to forgive ourselves. If we are still angry at ourselves for the "stupid" things we did as a child, we cannot respect ourselves as fully as we need to do in order to get the most out of life.

We know what we did; we were there the whole time. We do not want anyone to find out because it would be too humiliating. The pain of our guilt would be unbearable and we would be punished severely. We spend our lives preventing this exposure of our underlying feelings of worthlessness, but it gnaws at our heart every day.

Much of this scenario takes place below the level of conscious awareness. We must make it conscious so that it can be properly drained and healed, like an abcess. It is hard to do for ourselves, for we are too close to it. We need the intervention of a competent counselor.

There's the rub. If we tell a counselor what we did, our secret will be out and the wheels of retribution will start to turn. We cannot bring ourselves to set this process in motion -- it might hurt too much. This fear keeps many people from getting the help they need.

One response to this resistance to psychotherapy is that we can stand more pain now as adults than we could as children. Another response is that most of this psychic pain is fictitious. We are not guilty. We were merely imperfect human beings at the time as we are imperfect adults now. Our saving grace is that we are not worthless *because* of what happened. We are worthwhile *in spite of it.*

"Why did I let it happen?" Many of us suffer from terrible guilt over things that happened to us as children. Underneath our feelings of guilt, we are angry at the perpetrators of our victimization. We resist the conscious awareness of this anger because we are afraid of the consequences. We do not know what the consequences might be and we do not want to find out.

Deeper still is our anger at ourselves for letting it happen, as if a child could have prevented anything from happening in the real world. We imagine as children that we are responsible for everything that happens in our little world, and if something bad happens, we have no one but ourselves to blame. Not only do we feel responsible, guilty and ashamed, but we are angry at ourselves. We cannot respect anyone who fails to prevent such terrible things from happening.

These are all attitudes that we have about ourselves. They are mistaken attitudes and they must be replaced with better ones. We can effect this change in our self-attitudes by writing our feelings down on a piece of paper. First, we can write an anger letter to the perpetrator, who will never see it. Then, if we wish, we can write a cleaned-up version that we can send or not. It is our choice.

The next step is to write ourselves an anger letter. "If only I did this or that, the whole thing would not have happened. I should have seen it coming, I should have known. Why was I so stupid?" When we get these childhood misperceptions out where we can see them, we can begin the process of reevaluating them in the light of our adult intelligence and experience. We can see the absurdity of requiring ourselves as children to outwit older, stronger victimizers who should have known better than to take advantage of a situation but did not. We can see that these people did not respect themselves. They were behaving out of their self-contempt, and we hate them for it. But we didn't do it. We need not be angry at ourselves.

We can even find it in our hearts to forgive that little child for being so terribly inadequate to cope with a situation that children should not have had to cope with. We need to ask the question, *"What kind of children allow such terrible things to happen? Bad children? Immoral children? Guilty children? Stupid children?"* The answer, of course, is "none of the above." These things happen to imperfect children in an imperfect world, which is regrettable enough. We need not make it worse by condemning ourselves to a lifetime of grief and self-punishment for something we did not do and could not prevent.

Now that we have put our self-anger in this new perspective, we are ready to take the last step in the anger management process. We have a choice now: to hang onto our anger or to let it go. Our residual anger at ourself has been keeping us from being as happy as we deserve to be, it keeps us from being as loving as we can be, it keeps us from respecting ourself. And who is it up to to make this important, life-affirming choice? It is up to us.

Vignette: It's All My Fault

When Lisa came to therapy, she and David had just broken up. She felt that her life was falling apart. She was distraught and out of control. She cried all the time. Lisa found herself calling David forty times in one day; she couldn't stop herself.

Lisa was a very attractive, successful airline executive, but she could not achieve what was most important to her, a stable, happy relationship. David was number seven in a ten-year succession of emotional disasters. It was all very discouraging. Not only did she feel like a failure at the task of love, but she blamed herself for these disasters, which only compounded her distress.

When we asked Lisa what would she like to achieve most in therapy, her answer was, "People think I'm so good-looking and such a winner, but I feel like a fake. I have no real self-esteem. I'm so depressed and tired all the time. Each time I break up with someone, I just fall apart. I feel so weak and stupid for allowing this to happen to me over and over again. What is wrong with me? Maybe I could feel better about myself if I could just stop calling him."

As the oldest of four children, Lisa played the role of the responsible child and took care of her two brothers and handicapped sister. Lisa remembers that her mother was never there for her, but she had to be there for everybody else. To make matters worse, her mother resented the fact that her father showed Lisa attention.

From this upbringing, Lisa acquired the following attitudes:

"Helpers are not there to help me, so I conclude that I am not worth helping."

"If my own mother cannot love me, who can? Nobody. I am unlovable, I can be abandoned at any time."

"Nothing I do is good enough."

"I pretend to be strong but I'm really weak inside. My strongness is a fake and so am I."

"My hard work is not appreciated and I feel good for nothing; Since I am the responsible one, everything that goes wrong is my fault."

"When I fail, it proves that my parents were right. I really am worthless and unlovable and there's nothing I can do about it."

We pointed out to Lisa that each time a man leaves her, it confirms her old feelings of worthlessness. This confirmation undermines her feelings of accomplishment in the real world and keeps her from being happy. She holds herself in contempt. This gap between the reality of her business success and her underlying self-contempt is what makes her feel like a fake. Lisa feels powerless to do anything about this unhealthy family of hers, and in a crisis her old feelings of inadequacy come pouring back -- she falls apart.

Her heartache in the present is painful enough, but the apparent confirmation of her childhood feelings of worthlessness makes it even worse.

In our problem-solving process, we look for an entry into the individual's constellation of mistaken attitudes, convictions and expectations. Lisa's tale of woe provided us with many such points of entry such as "the helpers do not help," "I can be emotionally abandoned at any time," "I am inadequate to cope," "I am a fake," "I am unlovable," "My life is out of control and so am I" and "I feel good for nothing." We also know that Lisa is angry at herself for being so inadequate to solve her problems. But we chose to leave that issue for a later visit.

It's All My Fault

We felt that Lisa's pain was being compounded by her intense self-blame. She kept saying that everything is her fault. Her efforts to contact David were not so much to win back his love and affection as they were to relieve the pain of her guilt, fault and responsibility for what happened. She felt that she had to do something. She had no choice. Calling David was "doing something," even if it didn't make sense.

This tendency to blame herself for what goes wrong has been a recurring theme for the last twenty-eight years. It is instantaneous and nonrational. It is a bad habit. It needs to be replaced with better habits.

To strengthen Lisa's self-respect, we must give her homework. We do not simply say, "Lisa it is not your fault," because that would just prove to her that we do not understand how guilty and worthless she really feels. We do not point out to her that she gravitates to difficult, irresponsible men in order to confirm her negative attitudes toward herself. She would hear this as an accusation and would assume responsibility for this negative compatibility. We did not tell Lisa to stop calling David. That is not the issue. The issue was the self-contempt that prevented her from solving her own personal problems and forced her to depend on the judgment of people who were no more competent than she was. We do not do what she expects. We do not give her good advice which she would not take anyway. Instead, we do what she doesn't expect. We take her side, we agree with her.

"Maybe you are right Lisa. Maybe it is all your fault. What do you plan to do about it?"

"I have no idea, that's what I came to therapy for."

"Lisa, you have a choice now to hang on to this guilt, fault and blame or to let it go. What choice do you prefer?"

"I choose to let it go, of course, but how do I do that?"

"You are not as powerless and out of control as you think you are. You have the power to stand in judgment on Lisa forever and condemn her for her worthlessness and stupidity, or you can choose to forgive yourself."

"But it is me! I keep doing it. I have no one but myself to blame."

"We've already established that. That is not the problem. Would you like to break this cycle of fault leading to fault."

"Of course I would."

"What are you afraid would happen if you did?"

"I wouldn't know who I was."

"That's scary isn't it? And it is going to take courage to let go of the old Lisa and see who takes her place."

"I'm not sure I can do that."

"I agree. Of course you are not sure. If you were sure, it wouldn't take courage. You have the power of choice and you have the power to forgive. You can choose to use these powers to your advantage."

"I'm really tired of doing things for other people. Maybe it's time I did something for myself. Is that selfish? I always thought it was."

"It is not selfish at all. It is entirely appropriate that you take care of yourself for a change."

"How do I forgive myself? I just know I'm going to do it again, I can't seem to stop myself. I must be stupid or something."

"I agree that 'stupidness' is unforgivable. But that is not what you are. What you are is imperfect, and your imperfections set you up to make mistakes in judgment that you would not have made otherwise."

"But I'm too imperfect."

"Our goal is to make you less imperfect. Can you forgive yourself for being as imperfect as you have been all these years? You will soon learn that you did not get this way all by yourself. You had help."

"Do you mean that it's my parents' fault?"

"What if it is no one's fault? What if they were imperfect too, and taught you things about yourself that were not true? You have been behaving accordingly ever since. You are an obedient child. They ordered you to fail and you've been obeying that order since third grade."

"Maybe some day I will be able to forgive them, but I can't right now."

"That's true, but first you must learn to forgive yourself."

"What if I can't? What if I don't?"

"That is a 'what if.' You are predicting failure in the future based on your failures in the past. That is your discouragement talking. This is a new ball game. The new Lisa can choose to live in the present and do what reality requires right now."

Homework

Lisa did her homework. She wrote herself a forgiveness letter. As she saw the parade of sins, crimes, guilts and faults marching across the page, she was able to put them into a new perspective. These were not sins or crimes at all. They were human imperfections. She could see that some of her vulnerabilities came from her mother's unhappy example and that she was consistently gravitating to men who reminded her of her father, who didn't have much self-respect. She realized that hanging onto this history of disasters did not make things better, it only perpetuated her negative consistencies.

She had a new tool now, she had the power of choice. She could choose to hang on or let go. She was afraid that if she let these old consistencies go, she would not know who she was any more. But these griefs and regrets were not her identity; they were excess baggage from the past. She could choose to throw them overboard. She chose to let them go.

As she freed herself from these burdens, she felt liberated, independent, in control, appropriately responsible for herself and grown up. She no longer needed to depend on David for the validation of her worth as a person. That was the wrong solution to the wrong problem. It had nearly driven her crazy. Now, the whole problem had become fictitious and it did not need to be solved. She could validate her own existence now. She had an independent identity of her own. She did not call David forty times that day -- she was free of him and of the Lisa that she used to be.

As she looked over her forgiveness letter, she saw that she was not such a bad person after all and that other people were using her mistaken attitudes, roles and beliefs against her. Hanging onto her old guilts did not make her less vulnerable, as she had hoped; it made her more vulnerable. Respecting herself could make it easier to avoid guilt-producing situations in the future. Lisa was able to replace her guilt feelings with feelings of regret. She was sorry that these bad things had happened, and her regret was appropriate.

Lisa saw that blaming herself for everything was mischief-- it didn't need to be done and was counterproductive. She was able to disengage from her own self-destructive mischief. Lisa felt like an equal member of the human race in spite of her faults and imperfections. As an imperfect human being, she saw that there was nothing to forgive.

#34. GIVE IT A PASS

Some people think that they have only two choices: to respond to an anger provocation in kind like a stand-up guy or to slink off into the corner like a wimp. There is a third choice that we did not know we had -- to give it a pass.

Curly: "Your wife is ugly."

Moe: Shrug.

Curly: "Your kid is ugly."

Moe: Stare.

Curly: "You're ugly too."

Moe: Shrug. Stare.

This nonsense isn't worth responding to. It is a waste of our time and energy. We have chosen on an adult basis not to dignify it with a reply. We are not suppressing our anger. There was no real grievance here, only useless kid stuff. The anger did not ignite inside of us. There is no anger here to suppress. We are not letting them get away with murder. There is no murder, only mischief. We have no good intention to improve their deportment. We give them a pass for our benefit, not theirs. When they see that their mischief has failed to produce the desired overreation, they write us off and find another patsy.

#35. GIVE THEM A CHOICE

Most people express their anger the same way every time perhaps with sarcasm, revenge, sulking, pouting or screaming. They do not enjoy expressing their anger in these negative, destructive ways, but no one has ever told them what their options are. They have no choice, and that is frustrating in itself.

We can render a great service by revealing to our friends and loved ones that there are better ways to communicate their legitimate anger. We are not "giving" them a choice so much as we are revealing alternatives that they had all along but didn't know they had.

Vignette: It's up to You

Clare and Blanche had been friends since third grade. Blanche had always been known for her temper. She was just like her mother. Clare was more the long-suffering type, the pleaser who could not bring herself to tell people the truth about how she felt. In counseling, Clare learned how to tell her friend the unpleasant truth about their relationship. This was not a good intention to straighten Blanche out; she had a real intention for herself.

"Blanche, I'm sorry that you were so angry last night. I don't blame you for being angry, that's not the point. The point is the way you express it. For years, I've been telling myself, 'She doesn't really mean what she is saying. That's just the way Blanche is. She can't help herself.' But it hurt my feelings when you blew up like that. How would you feel if I talked to you that way?"

"I've never thought about it. It must be hard to take sometimes."

"It's hard to take all the time. It's not your fault. I realize now that no one ever told you what else you can do besides blow up all over the place."

"But I feel better after I let it all out. Isn't that what I'm supposed to do?"

"Do we have to eat a whole egg to know that it is spoiled?"

Rudolph Dreikurs

"You don't live on a desert island. There are other people involved, and you need to take their feelings into consideration. You have lost too many good friends already. Besides, your momentary relief doesn't change anything for the better. You will blow up again the next time you get angry."

"You're right. I've been doing this since grammar school. The rest of me has grown up, but this part hasn't."

"You have choices now that you don't know about. You can choose to express your anger in a less hurtful way."

"I don't know if I can change."

"It helps if you know what there is to change to. For instance, you can choose to say, 'It makes me angry when you do that,' or 'when that happens.' You can also choose to write an anger letter to the person you are angry at."

"What if I am angry at myself?"

"You have probably been angry at yourself for years. This underlying anger at yourself blows up in my face when I am ten minutes late for dinner. You can drain it out of your system by writing yourself an anger letter."

"That sounds so silly."

"It's no sillier than driving your friends away with that out-of-control temper of yours."

"What if I don't do it?"

"There's no law that says you have to write anger letters. These are choices that you have. These are preferences that have been open to you all your life. You just didn't know about them. You are not doing it for me or for our friendship. You are doing

it for you. It will give you some relief from your pent-up anger. It is up to you to do it or not. But if things don't get better, I will have to start seeing you less often. My heart can't take it anymore. If you blow up at me next Saturday night, I want you to know in advance that I'm not going to rationalize it away any more. It's just too unpleasant. I will just get up and go home."

"Is that a threat?"

"No, it's not a threat; it's just my preference. I'm not trying to control you for your own good. But I have a choice to stay or to leave. By staying around, I am giving you permission to abuse me, and that's not good for our relationship. I have my choices and you have yours. It is up to you now. I just want you to know in advance so that you won't be taken by surprise."

"I guess it's about time I stopped putting on a sideshow for everybody. I used to get what I wanted by throwing a tantrum, but I can see now that I have been paying too high a price for it. It's not worth it."

"You can choose to let it go and replace it with something more constructive like asking for what you want. As I said, it's not up to me. It's your choice; it's up to you."

#36. GRIEF AND LOSS

As Elizabeth Kubler-Ross writes in her book, **On Death and Dying,** there are four stages in the grieving process:

1. Denial -- "Oh no! It can't be true."

2. Anger -- "Why is this happening to me? It's so unfair."

3. Bargaining -- "I'll do anything."

4. Acceptance of the inevitable.

Many times, the acceptance stage does not take place. Instead, we have a feeling of resignation to our fate, which is not a healthy outcome at all. Resignation is malignant, and it will consume us if it is left untreated.

In our resignation, which includes the tendency to withdraw from the world in discouragement and say, "I give up, what's the use," there is an element of residual anger that has not been successfully worked through. This anger soon turns into depression, which contributes its unhealthy share to the malignant situation.

Anger is our natural response to a grievance, which includes the loss of a loved one. It is important that we apply some of the anger management techniques that we have learned in this book, but this is difficult to do because the anger component in our grief is often lost in the mixture of strong and deep emotions that we have been experiencing. Our anger gets away from us and it prolongs our grief. Even though we are not consciously aware of our anger as such, we need to ask ourselves some focusing questions, such as *"Who am I angry at?"* We never think of asking such questions because we all learned that we are not supposed to be angry at the person who died. That is not acceptable in polite society and is considered unseemly. We would feel too guilty, so we solve the problem by choosing to suppress our anger. Yet we are angry at them just the same, not for dying, but for causing us this bereavement. We are not blaming our loved one for dying, but we are legitimately angry that it happened. If we are angry at the deceased for leaving and abandoning us, for betraying our trust that they would live forever, we can write that emotion down in an anger letter. It is not a hate letter. We are merely expressing our anger in a mature, appropriate way in order to save our own sanity.

It is healthy for us to validate our own legitimate anger at our loss. Our focusing question often has the effect of making the facets of our unconscious, "unacceptable" anger conscious, so that we can resolve our conflicting attitudes and attain some relief.

The next focusing question might be, *"What angers me the most about this loss?"* The answer often bubbles up immediately. "It is so unfair. This is not supposed to happen to good people." We need to identify our vulnerability to perceive unfairness in situations where fairness is not a relevant consideration. Fairness does not have to do with rewarding goodness or punishing badness. Fairness means "without bias." These tragedies happen every day in an imperfect world and our mistake is to protest the cosmic unfairness of it all. We can use our adult sensibilities to put our anger in a more bearable perspective. Cosmic rage is unbearable and unmanageable.

Our response to the focusing question might be, "Why does this have to happen to me?" This response tells us that we are perceiving this regrettable loss as if it were a personal victimization, which it is not. We are not a victim, we are a worthwhile human being in spite of what has happened to us.

We can continue to ask ourselves, *"What else angers me the most about what happened?"* We can use our responses to shed some light on the powerful attitudes that are contributing to our distress and making our grief more painful than it needs to be. We may be angry at the wrongness of it all and standing in moral judgment of the responsible party or of the system. We may be angry that all of our goodness in the deceased person's behalf has been in vain and that we have been good for nothing. That is unfair, also. Our anger problem has many facets, and the more aspects of our anger that we can identify and relieve, the better off we will be. We will recover from our grief sooner than we would otherwise.

"Neither fight nor give in; cooperate instead."

Rudolph Dreikurs

The next focusing question is, *"Who else are we angry at?"* Perhaps we are angry at the doctors at the hospital, the drunk driver or some other individual who contributed to this loss. Now the question becomes, *"What can I do about it?"* When we feel that there is nothing we can do because revenge would only get us in more trouble, we feel powerless and out of control. This powerlessness is painful, and it compounds all of the other pain that we are feeling. We can relieve this component of our distress by choosing to write the object of our anger an anger letter. This is an action that we can take on our own behalf. It puts us back in touch with the real world. It helps us to break the cycle of negative feelings and emotions whirling inside of us and restores the feeling that we are in control, competent, independent and all the other facets of self-respect. We do not have to mail the letter. It is not for them -- it is for us.

What if we are angry at God? We can write the Deity an anger letter, too. What if we are angry at ourselves? We may blame ourselves for failing to prevent it or to get there in time. We may be obsessing about these unsolved and, by now, insoluble problems. We are in the throes of, "If only I had. . ." and we cannot get out.

Writing ourselves an anger letter often gives us some relief from our feelings that these problems are insoluble and that we are guilty as charged. We are not guilty; we are merely imperfect. The problems are not insoluble. They are, in most cases, fictitious problems that reality does not require us to solve.

#37. GOOD INTENTIONS MAKE US ANGRY

How do you feel when Aunt Birdy pushes more mashed potatoes on your plate and you have to lose six pounds by Saturday night? You feel angry. But you can't very well punch out a sweet old lady who only wants you to live forever.

You have a conflict. It is the same one that you have had for years. You either express your anger openly and risk losing an aunt, or suppress it again where it will turn into symptoms that you do not need. Fortunately for you, there is a third choice, the middle way:

1.   You can remember to identify Auntie's unwanted benevolence as mischief -- it does not need to be done. She is pleasing you her way, not your way.

2.   You can disengage emotionally from her mischief. You can choose not to perceive it as an insult to your intelligence and maturity, which it is not. You do not take it personally -- it isn't you, it's her.

3.   She is not your enemy and you are not her out-of-control victim. She is merely an imperfect human being and her imperfection is making you angry.

4.   You have a choice to manage your anger in the new way or manage it the same way you did when you were six.

5.   You can choose to consider the source and let your anger go. "It's only Aunt Birdy playing the only role she knows."

6.   You are now free to do the unexpected on your own terms as an independent grown-up. You can choose to validate the goodness of her intentions, not the content. You can say something like, *"I know that you want the best for me, Auntie, and I appreciate it, but I'll be fine."* You have just told the truth about yourself and about her. When she hears you talking to her in this new, more mature way, she will respect you and stop treating you like an overgrown six year old.

#38. GOOD FOR NOTHING

When we do good things for people, we expect something good in return such as a thank you, a smile or a nod. We feel disappointed when we do not get the reciprocity that we expect.

Some of us feel more than disappointed. We become angry at the unfairness of this ingratitude. We take the absence of validation as if it were an invalidation. Our goodness has been all for nothing. We feel that we were taken advantage of and played for a fool. We let it happen. We were stupid. We should have seen it coming and we failed to prevent it. Our "stupidity" makes us angry at ourselves. We feel like a chump, and it's our own fault.

These bad feelings, which constitute the "Good for Nothing Syndrome," make us feel worthless. They confirm our feelings of inferiority and inadequacy from childhood. We will learn nothing from our setback. We may say to ourselves, "No more Mister Nice Guy," but we will do it all over again tomorrow.

Antidote

Our antidote to feeling good for nothing, which means worthless, is our self-respect. *"I am a worthwhile human being in spite of my faults and imperfections, whether you appreciate me or not. I am not dependent on you for my worth as a person. I can validate my own goodness. I know what I did. I behaved appropriately under the circumstances. I would not have behaved any other way. I need not be angry at myself."*

#39. HARVEY WALLBANGER

The Harvey Wallbanger solution to the anger problem involves the perforation of plaster walls, doors, partitions and other structural materials with one's fist, head, foot or feet. The individual, usually a male, is trying to express his anger without doing bodily harm to his loved ones and other persons who could file charges. He may imagine that these outbursts give him relief from his anger, but such relief from super-anger can only be partial and temporary. The adrenalin will continue to pump, and his anger will continue to build in his psyche until some minor irritant triggers the next eruption. He has not broken his anger

HARVEY WALLBANGER

down into its components. He has not identified the real object of his anger, which is probably himself. Someone ought to reveal to him that he has other choices that won't be so hard on the wallpaper.

#40. THE HAT TRICK, OR VOTING WITH YOUR FEET

Someone once said that the best way to win a fight is with your hat -- grab it and run. There is a certain amount of truth in that unlovely homily, and it is nice to know that flight is one of our legitimate options. We are not required to go down with the ship in the name of "perseverance."

There is no law that requires you to state your case over and over ten times after your point has been shouted down the last nine times. When you see that you are getting nowhere, that both of you are temporarily out of control, you have the power of choice: You can choose to say it for the eleventh time or you can choose to grab your hat and run.

When you choose to leave the arena, you are allowing a number of positive things to happen: You are giving your respective wounds time to heal; you are giving both parties a chance to come down from their highly charged emotional state; and you are allowing your adult competence and judgment to come to the surface in a calmer atmosphere.

This is not "quitting" or "wimping out." This is assuming appropriate responsibility for resolving a problem that was not being resolved any other way. This is not withdrawal in discouragement, but disengaging from mutual mischief. This is not abdicating responsibility, but appropriate responsibility for your own sanity. This is true control. You are making it happen on your own valid terms.

#41. HOW DOES THAT HELP?

Believe it or not, your tormentor Ralph may be inflicting his anger upon you for your own good. He is hoping to pound some sense into your thick skull and you don't even appreciate it. He only wants you to be better than you are. In addition, he is screaming at his six-year-old daughter in order to improve her deportment and ridiculing his nine-year-old son in order to make a man of him. He actually thinks he is helping! He is not thinking at all, of course. These good intentions of his have nothing to do with being rational. They are attitudes that formed in the matrix of his relationship with his own parents and siblings, who didn't know what they were doing either.

That is why we do not make the mistake of saying, "Stop that, you're hurting Billy's feelings." In Ralph's own nonrational view, hurting feelings is supposed to help develop self-reliance, so why should he stop?

No one has ever questioned the "helpfulness" of these destructive behaviors. We do not attack the behavior because "parenting skills" is not Ralph's issue. His issue is phony helpfulness to his child as his ill-prepared father was helpful to him. On a deeper level, he is using this "helpful" good intention to overcompensate for his painful feeling that he was inadequately prepared for the task of parenting. When his imperfect child breaks a two-dollar coffee cup, it reactivates his underlying conviction that he does not know how to cope. This reactivation is painful. Ralph is trying to relieve the pain of this reminder of his own inability to cope at his child's expense. He is trying to help himself, but he doesn't know how to do that either. He is helping no one. It is all counterproductive mischief.

Our technique here is to zero in on the "helpfulness" aspect of his mischievous good intentions; not in a threatening or judgmental way, nor as a partisan in the child's behalf against his father, but in a conciliatory, thought-provoking way.

"Ralph, how does that help?"

He may or may not answer our question. He may not know what to say. That is all right. At least we have started him thinking. In a sense, it is a rhetorical question. We do not expect an answer. This is our way of planting a seed of doubt in our co-parent's mind and opening a window to let in some fresh winds of change.

#42. HUMOR

No book on anger management could be complete without at least a mention of humor as an outlet for hostility, which is a high-tech name for the emotion of anger.

We understand behavior in terms of its purpose. Humor is behavior, and it can have many purposes. Some purposes are negative and some are positive depending on the predisposition of the humorist:

1. Making a joke is "doing something" when there isn't much else that we can do to relieve the pent-up pressure of our anger. It relieves our feelings of powerlessness and gives us a choice that we would not have otherwise.

2. A joke often represents a compromise between saying something dangerously displeasing and saying nothing at all. It is a third choice.

3. A humorous put-down can be a subtle way of getting revenge on a mischief maker who cannot be attacked openly.

4. Humor is a form of self-empowerment. "I have the power to say this funny thing and you can't stop me."

5. Humor may have an element of superiority -- "I have the ability to see the absurdity of this situation and you do not."

This does not make humor pathological in itself. If we are healthy, self-respecting human beings, our humor will be a saving grace, a lightening of the situation for everyone's benefit. However, if we are suffering from unresolved residual anger from the past, our humor will be hurtful and destructive. If we are suffering from extreme self-contempt, we will find humor in cruelty and pain.

Humor, like every other human attribute, does not exist in a vacuum; it exists in a human context. Its purposes will be consistent with that context. As people replace their childhood self-contempt with self-respect, they find themselves able to resist the temptation to say something funny at someone else's expense. They can choose to let the opportunity pass. They do not miss it.

Vignette: Humor Is in the Ear of the Beholder

Lily and Ron had been going together for a year. Lily's job took her out of town overnight. Ron didn't like the idea of her being alone at night in a hotel full of travelling salesmen. He had been burned many times before. He trusted Lily, but he didn't trust her travelling companions.

Lily had the habit of "teasing" Ron about his suspicions. She would call from the hotel and make little jokes about male-female goings-on, and Ron would bite every time. His old jealousies would rise up in him and he would be in a lot of pain. He told Lily to stop, but she didn't see why she should.

The Wednesday before their counseling session, Lily called from Tucson to say that her sales presentation for the regional director was a hit." It was another notch on my bedpost, I mean, a feather in my cap." She had done it again. Ron's old angers at past betrayals came to the surface. He knew that the issue wasn't Lily's conduct, but his vulnerability to being provoked. However, he could not sort out his angers at her for doing this to him either from his anger at the last three women in his life or from his anger at his mother. They used to provoke him terribly, also. He always seemed to gravitate toward women who made him angry.

When asked why she made jokes knowing that Ron was sensitive to the issue of betrayal, Lily said, "I just want him to make me feel attractive to other men when I am so far away from home."

This answer tells us that Lily's "joke" has the purpose of relieving her feelings of inferiority and insecurity. It reveals a core of dependency behind her facade of corporate success. Below these purposes, there is a still deeper one. It isn't that Lily "forgets" how much she hurts Ron with her amusing shots. She remembers very well. She wants to have it both ways. She wants to hurt him and get away with it. Why does she want to hurt him? She is angry at him for being jealous, which she sees as controlling and demeaning. It is hard for her to express her anger directly, so she uses "innocent" remarks as her way of getting revenge. It works all too well. Ron's anger at these provocations turns into thoughts of betrayal and victimization. He listens to her phone conversations not to reassure himself that she is all right, but to try to find "clues" as to what she is really doing behind his back. He has begun to feel like a persecuted victim of women, which is a role he learned to play in his mother's house. His anger has turned into paranoia. That hurts.

When Lily comes home, Ron is not glad to see her. He is still smoldering. Lily's self-serving mischief has turned out to be counterproductive, as it usually does.

Lily's homework is to tell Ron that his insecurities make her angry. She is to catch herself depending on Ron for the validation of her femininity and choose to validate her own worth as a person instead. When she thinks about it, she sees that her "jokes" never did accomplish their "purpose" of making her feel more attractive. She can do much better without them.

Ron's homework is to catch himself falling for Lily's mischief and taking it personally as a confirmation of his old role as a victim. The new Ron is a worthwhile human being in spite of his imperfections, both past and present. Lily is a worthwhile human being in spite of her imperfections, too. If she makes him angry, he is not to say, "Stop telling me jokes like that," which would be giving orders. He cannot secure her cooperation that way. Instead, he can choose to say, *"It makes me angry when you pick my scabs and make them bleed."* There is nothing funny about that.

Ron's additional homework is to trust Lily. Before he can do that, he needs to trust himself more. He is the one who chose her for his companion. He made a good choice. He just didn't make a perfect one. He is worthwhile in spite of it.

Do's and Don't's

Do not cloak your anger in a funny remark. People are not deceived. They are hurt by your anger, whether it is said in fun or not. "I was only kidding, can't you take a joke?" Yes, they can, but that was not a joke. If you are angry, tell the truth. If there is an absurdity in the situation, you can comment on that without attacking the other individual personally. For instance:

When they say	You can say
"You are stupid."	*"I was absent that day.*
"Why haven't you walked the dog yet?"	*"You can't get good help."*
"You're too sensitive."	*"What should I be, insensitive?"*
"You're just like your father."	*"Whose father should I be like?"*
"Why on earth did you do that?"	*"It seemed like a good idea at the time."*

Do not use humor or sarcasm against a child. A child looks to you for validation and encouragement. A child is no match for your verbal fluency and can only come out of the exchange a loser -- inferior and discouraged. The child takes what you say more personally than you realize. Just because it happened to you in your childhood, you do not have a license to pass the damage onto the next generation.

#43. "I" MESSAGE

When we are angry, we are quick to focus on the person who provoked us. Our attention is directed towards the person who caused our grievance. We are predisposed to relieve the pain of our anger at the other person's expense. We are trying to build ourselves back up by tearing them down. We say things like, "You should do this" or "You should stop doing that." Our speech is full of advice, commands, condemnations and recriminations, none of which is constructive.

We need to be smarter than that. We need to stop sending counterproductive "you" messages and begin to talk about ourselves. We are in no position to read another person's mind, to understand their underlying purposes or to assess this unpleasant situation logically and dispassionately. We feel inadequate to cope with it. When we talk to other people about themselves, we get into deep water that we cannot always get out of again.

We are much better off talking about ourselves. We are experts on ourselves -- we know how we feel, we know what happened to make us feel that way and we have preferences as to what we plan to do in the future. We can choose to express our anger in the middle ground between ranting and stuffing. For instance, we can say, *"It makes me angry when you do that. I am very angry right now. If it happens again, I will be angry again. I just want you to know how I feel. If you don't want me to feel this way any more, you know what your choices are. It is up to you."*

When we talk about ourselves, we are not moralizing, judging or criticizing. We are not provoking a counterreaction that nobody wants. We are telling the truth. We are creating an opportunity for a dialogue between two imperfect human beings, one of whose imperfections made the other angry. The damage is not irreparable and the mistake is not fatal, so let us clear the air so that we can get on with our lives.

When we talk about ourselves, we are helping the other person to understand us in an appropriate way. We are revealing ourselves in ways that will help them to cooperate with us in the future. We are not giving orders or demanding submission. If we use the right words and the right music, as self-respecting human beings in our own right, we will make the relationship stronger than it was before.

"Courage is the willingness to take a risk. "

Rudolph Dreikurs

"Do what you can do."

Rudolph Dreikurs

#44. I'M SORRY

Some people find it difficult to use the words, "I am sorry." These words seem to imply some sort of guilt, and they are reluctant to make that painful admission.

"I am sorry," does not imply a confession of culpability at all. It means, "I regret that this negative thing happened." You are not "owning" the problem or assuming responsibility for solving it. You merely feel appropriate regret that whatever happened, happened. You are also expressing regret that the other person is in so much pain. If that is truly how you feel, then that is what you say. This is called "Telling the Truth."

"I'm sorry," is particularly hard for perfectionists to say. It is a painful exposure of their failure to achieve total perfection. They want to keep such failures a secret forever. When you say "I'm sorry," it is your way of giving yourself permission to be an imperfect human being -- a permission that your parents and teachers may never have given you. You are an adult now and it is time that you gave it to yourself. As you will see throughout these pages, it is all right to be imperfect, you are worthwhile in spite of it.

"I'm sorry," is a very effective anger management technique. It takes the sting out of the situation. It is like putting salve on a burn. It focuses appropriate attention on the emotional component of the other person's distress and away from the superficial debate about who did what to whom. Very often, if you do it right, you will get an, "I'm sorry, too," in return. What could be better than that?

#45. LET IT GO

"As a self-respecting human being, I can choose to hang onto this grievance or I can choose to let it go. Hanging on never helped,

123

but maybe letting go will."

"I am not powerless and out of control."

"I have the power of choice."

"I can choose to let it go."

"I do not need this aggravation."

"I don't need this power struggle."

"I don't need to control this situation."

"I don't need to straighten this other person out."

"I don't have to solve this problem because it isn't worth solving. It is only mischief."

"I have other things to do with my time and energy. I am not quitting or copping out. I am just letting it go. I'm letting it go not from weakness, but from strength."

We are afraid to let go because we think that it means giving up control. Very often, when we let go of these worries, doubts and negative expectations, we will feel more in control than we even did before.

#46. LEX TALIONIS

One of the earliest attempts to manage anger was the Lex Talionis or Law of Retaliation: "A life for a life, an eye for an eye, a tooth for a tooth" (Exodus 21:24). To our modern taste, these prescriptions for counterdamages seem bloodthirsty and barbaric, but when we compare this enlightened agenda with the unlimited retaliation that preceded it, we can see that it was a step in the right direction. It was a daring breakthrough in social engineering. We might even say that the Lex Talionis was an early attempt to replace unbridled, out-of-control revenge with a primitive system of logical consequences. Anger management did not end there, it began there.

#47. LIGHTEN UP

It is very hard to be jovial when we are angry. When our adrenal glands are pumping adrenalin into our bloodstream, our digestive system shuts down and so does our sense of humor. Some of us never had a sense of humor to shut down. We go through life as though the present were something to be gotten over with as soon as possible. These people call themselves "serious," while we call them killjoys. Some people are at the other extreme. They see the humor in life even when there is no humor to be seen. They call themselves "optimistic" or "Susie Sunshine." We call them inane. They need to "lighten down." Here again, the goal is to find a healthy balance between too much cheerfulness and too little.

When you are in the grip of an anger attack, you can catch yourself perceiving the situation as grimmer than it really is. It is helpful if you can find an absurdity that you can both agree on such as, *"We sound like the second act of 'Aida,' don't we?"* See if that doesn't make the anger more manageable.

Vignette: Two Agendas in One Kitchen

Mike and Tina were fighting about the mess in the kitchen. Mike was perceiving her criticisms as if they were victimizations and he was defending himself against her. Tina was defending herself against his defenses. She was feeling unappreciated and unloved. Each one was recapitulating the stormy tenor of their parents' marriages and they hated it. Tina saw that she was getting nowhere with her good intentions to teach Mike the niceties of domestic management. He was not a willing pupil. So she decided to lighten up.

In the past, she had tried to end these anger spasms with a cute remark, such as, "You look so adorable when you scootch up your face like that." Mike was not mollified by these peace gestures. Indeed, he took them as further proof of his wife's lack of seriousness.

Tina chose to stop trying to lighten Mike up, which she had no competence to do, and to work on lightening up her own disposition instead. She was replacing her good intentions for Mike with a real intention for herself. She broke her heaviness down into its components so that she could let go of each one in turn:

1. *"Here I am, just like my mother, standing in moral judgment on my husband for his 'wrongness.' Who am I to judge another person's worth? Besides, it's hard work. I can choose to stop doing it."*

2. *"I am trying to improve my husband against his will. I can choose instead to accept him as he is, in spite of the fact that he has a long way to go. Maybe if I get off his back, he will improve himself."*

3. *"I am saying negative, hurtful things to the man I love. How can I build him up that way? I can choose to say something constructive instead, like, 'I'm sorry I yelled at you, let's have some hot chocolate'."*

4. *"I am defending my integrity in ways that do not work. I can choose to accept myself in spite of my unfortunate contribution to this confrontation. As an imperfect human being, I am not required to defend myself. I can stop any time I want."*

5. *"I am not the powerless victim of this hulk. I am not a pleasing child either. I have the power of choice. I can choose to stop doing what displeases me, like fighting, and to start doing what pleases me, like walking away."*

6. *"I am trying to wean Mike away from his parents' horrible example. I can't do that by screaming at him. I can do it by setting an example of self-respect for him to follow if he chooses. If I don't set it, he can't follow it. I am not doing this for his good -- I am doing it for my good."*

Tina said, *"I don't want to fight with you. I'm sorry I made you so angry. I'm going to make something to drink."* Mike yelled, "Come back here, I'm not through with you." *"Well, I am through with this fight. You can carry on without me."*

After a few more moments of grousing for the record, Mike got out the marshmallows and the cups. He cleared a space on the table and tried to remember why he overreacted to Tina's observation about his messiness. He realized that he was feeling like a victim, just as he did when his mother yelled at him for the same offense twenty years before. *"At least I'm consistent,"* he mused, *"It's hard to lighten up when you're being victimized. But I'm not a victim, I'm just a slob. I can live with that, but it certainly isn't worth defending or making either Tina or me unhappy over. Like Tina says, I'm a worthwhile human being in spite of my messiness. I think I'm starting to believe it."*

#48. LITIGATION

We do not have duels to the death anymore. Instead, we have instituted an even more painful technique of anger management called the lawsuit. We are the most litigious nation on earth. Our lawyers are the beneficiaries of our inability to solve anger problems like grown-ups. It would be much cheaper for all of us if we could learn to remove the anger component that turns a difference of opinion into a legalized grudge match. If we can identify our vulnerabilities to taking the ups and downs of life personally, we would be likelier to resolve disputes on a business-like basis in an atmosphere of mutual respect.

"The best way to destroy an enemy is to make him your friend."

Abraham Lincoln

#49. LOGICAL CONSEQUENCES

When we let our nonrational emotions determine our behavior, there is usually a price to pay. Our actions turn out to be counterproductive. Our emotions are a legitimate part of the human condition, but they have no brains. We have brains, but our emotions and feelings do not. Our feelings are important to us and we should know them by their rightful names, but they are not necessarily a reliable guide to taking actions in the real world. We need to interpose conscious thought and ask ourselves a focusing question or two, such as, *"What does the reality of the situation require us to do?"* Reality never requires us to behave irrationally, but we do it anyway. We have never learned how not to.

This is especially true when we are angry. Our predisposition and not our instinct is to relieve the pain of our anger. We need to replace this mindless predisposition to react impulsively with a more constructive predisposition. We can acquire the predisposition to replace our current system of illogical consequences such as yelling, screaming, hitting, sulking and so on with consequences that have some logical relation to the grievance in question.

For instance, when Susiebelle spills her orange juice, we consciously choose not to scold her and send her to her room. Nor do we lecture her on the evils of waste. We can say, *"It makes me angry when you knock over your orange juice. Get a sponge from the sink and clean it up."*

Susiebelle can see the logical connection between the antecedent and its consequence. She is not being held in contempt. She is merely an imperfect child with imperfect small muscle skills. Her imperfection does not make us super-angry. It only makes us angry and we tell her the truth in a way that does not deprive her of her self-respect.

This is how children learn about cause and effect. This is how the world works: If you make a mistake, it is your responsibility to repair the damage insofar as you are able to do so. Your worth as a person is not at stake -- it is not even an issue.

Logical consequences are not subjective, they are objective. Unlike punishment, they have the following characteristics:

1. Logical consequences express the reality of the social order, not solely that of the person applying them.

2. Logical consequences are logically related to the misbehavior.

3. Logical consequences involve no element of moral judgment.

4. Logical consequences are applied in a respectful manner.

5. Logical consequences are concerned only with what will happen now.

6. The child is given a choice and is informed of the consequences of his or her decision.

The prerequisite for imposing these logical consequences is self-respect. Self-respecting parents do not take the child's little misbehavior personally, for they are worthwhile in spite of it. They are free to use their adult judgment and their mature creative facilities to devise an appropriate and instructive consequence to impose upon the child. If the child abuses a privilege, the privilege is taken away. Toys left underfoot are put up on the closet shelf for an agreed-upon length of time. We do not deprive the child of our love and affection. That is not logical. We can be angry and love the child at the same time.

If we do not respect ourselves as much as we would like, we may use an anger situation as an opportunity to do some emotional growing up. We can catch ourselves about to overreact in the old destructive way and consciously choose not to. We can catch ourselves in the act, take a time out and give ourselves an opportunity for something more creative to bubble up. We are not merely counting to ten, but using this interval creatively to solve the problem at hand. To help us in our creative process, we can ask ourselves if the behavior was an honest mistake or mischief. If it is mischief, we can disengage from it, as we have learned to do and do the unexpected. They usually do not expect us to be logical. We can choose to do what they do not expect.

In any case, the old, nonlogical way never worked. We may have thought that "success" meant terrifying our children into silent submission. This is not positive success but is rather negative success. We have not solved any problems or even dealt with them intelligently. We have merely postponed them. Tyrannism is not logical.

If we can come up with a logical consequence, such as telling the truth, *"It makes me angry when you do that,"* which is always a good fallback position, we will experience a feeling of relief. We have confronted a problem in the real world and dealt with it constructively. We have earned the right to have feelings of accomplishment, success, competence, trust in our judgment, identity, maturity and control. Each time we do such homework, these positive feelings about ourselves get stronger. We are not building ourselves up by tearing anyone down. If we do it right, everyone wins and no one loses.

#50. MIND READING

Some of us expect our loved ones to read our minds. Rationally, we know that they cannot do it, but subjectively, we expect them to do it just the same. This expectation sets us up for a lifetime of frustration and disappointment. It is especially malignant in the area of anger management.

Vignette: You Should Know How I Feel

Mona and Bill were referred to the Anger Clinic by their marriage counselor. They fought all the time and it was destroying their relationship. It was clear that they could not get to their problems because their fulminating anger always got in the way.

The morning before their third session, they had a typical squabble. Mona said to him, "You're brushing your teeth too hard. You'll make your gums bleed." Bill defended his right to brush his teeth as hard as he pleased. The war was on. They would have a lot to talk about when they got to the clinic.

We began our analysis by asking our usual focusing question, *"What angered you the most?"*

Bill replied that Mona was trying to control him as usual and he resented it. He rebelled against her attempt to change him in ways that didn't make any sense.

Mona was only trying to help Bill and he did not appreciate her concern for his dental health. She felt good for nothing. She was angry at him and angry at herself for even trying to make his life better.

Mona, of course, had good intentions and they were an insult to Bill's intelligence. They made him angry.

Our next focusing question to Bill was, *"What angered you the most?"*

Bill didn't hesitate for a second, "She should have known that I was angry, but she kept going on and on about my gums."

"The issue is not gums, is it? The issue is that you were angry at her for inflicting her good intentions upon you without your permission. What does that mean, 'She should have known I was angry'?"

"It means she should have stopped doing what she was doing. She should have seen that I was angry at her."

"But she didn't. She had her own agenda. She was not attuned to yours. Where does that come from, this expectation that Mona should know that you are angry and be guided accordingly?"

"I don't know."

"What is the first thing you remember from your childhood?"

"My dad was a waiter in a strip joint. Mother hated it. They fought about it all the time. She was jealous. He said he needed the money. I remember one time they were punching each other in the living room, I was in the kitchen."

"How were you feeling?"

"Frightened and insecure. I couldn't express my feelings. I felt out of control. I remember thinking that if they only knew what they were doing to my insides, they would stop fighting."

"Did they ever find out what they were doing to your insides?"

"No, of course not."

"You never told them, did you? On what day did you stop hoping that people would read your mind and stop misbehaving without your having to tell them?"

"On no day. I guess I never did stop feeling that way."

"This morning, you were angry at Mona for her utter failure to read your mind and stop nagging you about your tooth-brushing style."

"Yes, I was. It all came back to me, feeling powerless and out of control, and still unable to tell her how I felt or what I wanted her to do."

"What do you think you might do about it the next time Mona makes you angry with her good intentions?"

"I don't know."

"You are right. You don't know. It is foreign to your upbringing. You have never seen two mature adults expressing their anger appropriately and solving their mutual problems cooperatively. It is no wonder that you feel inadequately prepared to solve your anger problems with Mona."

"I blame her for starting it, but underneath I know it's my fault."

"Does 'faulting' on yourself help? It is not a matter of fault. It is a matter of human imperfection. You were inadequately prepared to cope with these problems. It is not your fault."

"Is it my parents' fault?"

"It is no one's fault. We are all imperfect human beings and we make mistakes. Let's find out what they are so that we can stop making them."

"All right. What can I do next time?"

The first step is to identify your feeling. You cannot express your feeling if you do not know what it is. You are not 'upset.' You are angry."

"I was angry all right."

"The next step is to catch yourself expecting Mona to pick up on your vibrations. That is not her job. She has her own problems. She is not a mind reader. You have to read your own mind."

"I can do that."

"The third step is to express your anger appropriately. You can choose to say, 'Mona, it makes me angry when you tell me what to do.' Is that the truth?"

"Yes, that's the truth."

"Your homework then is to tell the truth about yourself. When you do, you will not feel controlled by Mona, you will be in control of yourself. You will be making it happen."

"Is it all right to tell her I'm angry?"

"Mona, is it all right if he says he is angry?"

"Of course it is. I would understand and calm down. I would know where you were coming from."

"I thought it would make you angry."

"It makes me angry when I don't know what's going on. I

don't think about your anger. I am too busy thinking about myself."

"What's the first thing you remember, Mona?"

"I remember feeling hurt and sad. I don't know why. One afternoon I was in my room, crying on my bed. Mother came in and said, 'What's wrong?' I was so hysterical I couldn't tell her. She said, 'If you can't tell me, I'm going to leave.' I couldn't tell her and she left. I cried even harder."

"How did you feel?"

"I felt abandoned. It was my fault. I couldn't tell her what she wanted."

"Are you afraid that Bill will abandon you too?"

"I never realized it, but you're right. That's why I try so hard to please him, so that he won't leave me."

"You are trying too hard in ways that work in reverse. You are driving him away from you with your good intentions."

"What else can I do instead? I have to do something."

"You can replace your good intentions with real intentions. You can do what reality requires, not what you think it requires."

"What's a real intention?"

"Telling the truth about your anger would be a real intention. Just like Bill, you cannot express your feelings to this day. You have a lot in common. Tomorrow morning, if Bill makes you angry. . ."

"I'm sure he will."

"I want you to catch yourself swallowing your anger for fear of being abandoned. You have Mona now, and as long as you have you, you cannot be abandoned."

"I'm not sure."

"It will be scary. You will have to take a risk. What will it take to tell him you are angry tomorrow?"

"It will take courage."

"What does courage mean?"

"I don't know."

"Courage is the willingness to take a risk."

"But maybe I don't want him to know I'm angry. He might leave."

"Bill, when she is screaming in your face, do you know she is angry?"

"It's hard to miss."

"So you see, Mona, your anger is not a secret. That is not the problem. Your problem is not Bill, you are the problem. You have an emotion that you cannot manage appropriately. You had better solve that problem before you worry about Bill's gums."

"What should I do?"

"Your homework is the same as Bill's. You can say, 'I'm angry at you,' or 'It makes me angry when you do that'."

"You're right. We need to communicate more."

"You need to replace your negative communications with positive communications. You need to change the words and the music."

"We need to tell the truth."

"I can do that."

"As you do your homework, you will be unlearning the miserable lessons that you learned about yourselves as children. You will replace your feelings of inadequacy with the feelings that you are competent to take life as it comes and solve problems as they arise. You will feel in control, independent and appropriate responsibility for yourself. You will even feel relief from the pressure of your pent-up anger. You will feel like equal members of the human race who can cooperate with each other in an atmosphere of mutual respect."

"We have no models of cooperation to follow."

"Starting now, you can learn to become your own models."

"We can do that."

"Don't forget, no more expecting Mona to read your mind and then complaining when she can't."

#51. MINIMIZE CONTACT

One very simple-sounding technique for managing the anger in our lives is to identify the people who provoke us the most and stay away from them.

As usual, this solution is not as simple as it seems. Neighbors have been known to shoot each other because of a fence a few inches over the property line. It is hard to stay away from people who live so close to us. We can use the technique of disengaging from their mischief. We can also reduce the time we spend in their company to a bare minimum. We do not have to waste hours of our lives listening to them scream insults in our face. We are in control of our feet and we can use them to walk away.

It is hard to minimize contact at work, but here too, we can choose to minimize our exposure to the boors and fools who clog up the hallways and elevators. We are not required to return insult for insult, nor to make them understand the error of their ways. We can choose to find other things to do with our time.

This is not "ignoring," "avoiding" or "copping out." We are using our adult judgment to make appropriate choices in the real world.

The same technique can be applied to relatives. We can see them when there is a family celebration or holiday, but we do not have to overdo it. We need not live in fear of displeasing them or of their gossip about us to the neighbors. We can choose to liberate ourselves from these carryovers from our childhood.

In American psychology, this solution would be seen as "running away from the problem" or "failing to confront the issue head on." We would say that every issue does not need to be confronted and resolved. We can use our adult intelligence to tell us where to best invest our time and energy. We have done our homework with these people and set an example of self-respect for them to follow if they choose. We can see that they are not responding to treatment and so we are off the hook. They may be too far gone in their self-contempt to be turned around now. We have reached the conclusion that these mischief makers are not there for us and we are not required to be there for them.

The Mother-Maker Syndrome

If we have been going back home time after time, spending years of our lives trying to make our female parent into a warm loving mother, then we need to examine our own motivations. This is a self-serving good intention, and it will not work the way we want it to. We are not accepting our parent the way she is but are trying to improve her for selfish reasons of our own. The same principles apply to male parents and siblings. When we replace our good intentions for these people with more appropriate intentions for ourselves, we will find it easier to minimize our contact with people who take more out of our lives than they put into it.

We are not giving up in discouragement. We are just making more appropriate arrangements for ourselves, which we have every right to do. We are not selfish or negative. We are minusing a minus in our lives. That is not a minus; it is a plus.

#52. NUMBING OUT

Some people complain of feeling "numbed out," "trapped in a void." They feel "cold" and "frozen." It is a painful, scary sensation. They feel terribly out of control because they do not know how they got into this state nor how to get out of it. This "numbed out" state can last for hours, days or weeks. Such people may be able to put on a facade of competence and carry on their normal activities without revealing to others their underlying distress.

Herman is suffering from the "Numbed Out Syndrome." His hypercritical mother ridiculed and scorned everything he did. He was a good boy, but a little uncoordinated. Mother praised his younger brother, Carl, who could do no wrong. Little Herman was in pain from his feelings of inadequacy to cope. He couldn't do anything about anything.

"I have cast my bread upon the waters and it didn't come back toasted."

Rudolph Dreikurs

His solution to the problem was to do nothing and feel nothing. His goal was not to achieve happiness, but to prevent further pain. His motto became, "Nothing ventured, nothing lost."

To this day, Herman feels that he cannot and dare not confide in anyone. He has learned from childhood that when he is emotionally distressed, the people that he counted on to help him-- his parents -- will turn against him and make his situation even worse. He has acquired the conviction that the "helpers do not help." He may also have concluded that he must be "strong" and "self-reliant." He must work these things out for himself like a "man," which, of course, he does not have the emotional preparation to do. He is the prisoner of this good intention that he has for himself. Herman has not resorted to alcohol or drugs to relieve the pain of his existence. He is doing it cold sober. He is "controlling" his way through life, numbing himself out from the inside.

As a consequence of these counterproductive attitudes, Herman has sealed himself off from other human beings. The worse it gets, the worse he gets. No wonder he feels trapped. He has defined control in terms of hanging on and keeping it all in. He has become a walking "black hole," letting nothing out and getting no relief from the mounting pressure of his counterproductive efforts to control his situation.

The day may come when the facade cracks. He can't keep it in and he can't let it out. He has an insoluble conflict. He may let go altogether and go berserk. He may kill someone or he may kill himself. His neighbors will say, "I don't understand it. He seemed normal yesterday."

This state can be understood as the consequence of mismanaged anger. The individual who does not respect himself has learned to feel that he is invalid and that his emotions are invalid, wrong and stupid. He has to deny the existence of such "worthless" emotions. Herman has spent twenty years learning to deny the validity of his anger. He does such a good job of denying it that he can't find it anymore. It gets away from him. He loses sight of the connection between his legitimate anger on Monday, his cold fury on Tuesday and his numbed out feeling on Wednesday. He has an emotion trapped inside of him that will not go up or down. He does not have a handle on it. He cannot manage it. In these extreme cases, the individual has gone beyond suppressing the experience of his painful anger. He has generalized his suppression and invalidation processes to all feelings and emotions. He has numbed himself out across the board.

Antidote

Once again, the antidote to the numbed out feeling is to restore the connection between the individual's present distress and the original precipitating anger. We can do that by asking our focusing questions. *"Who are you angry at? What happened to make you angry?"* Since he has lost sight of his anger, he may have to be prompted to remember. *"What happened yesterday? What happened the day before?"* You continue until his memory is jogged into making the connection. We need to be patient. His anger has congealed and it will take time to thaw out. In the meantime, we are creating an atmosphere in which he feels encouraged to express his anger for the first time in twenty years. We may even have to lead him by the hand by saying something like, *"It must have made you angry when your boss told you to do your whole report over."*

The next step is to hear him out and let him vent the anger that was not vented at the time it happened. In encouraging him to express his anger in detail, we are overcoming his tendency to deny his rage without even realizing that he has done so. It is a bad habit, and he can learn to replace it with a better one.

By our actions and our example in hearing him out in an atmosphere of mutual respect, we are canceling out, to a small extent, the lessons and attitudes that he learned so many years ago. He is experiencing contrary lessons in the present moment:

1. *"Some helpers do help."*

2. *"It's all right to get angry and to express it openly."*

3. *"The world will not come to an end if I let my feelings out."*

4. *"Control does not mean suppressing and denying. It means taking life as it comes, and that includes taking anger-provoking situations as they come and dealing with them in the present."*

5. *"I am not alone and abandoned in my time of distress. I have me and I am a member of the human race."*

6. *"I do not have to solve these problems all by myself to prove how independent and strong I am. I can ask for help when I need it, just like everyone else."*

7. *"I am an acceptable human being in spite of my unpleasant human emotions."*

8. *"I do not have to prove how strong I am by keeping my emotions in. As strong as I am, that is strong enough."*

Herman is now able to use his anger problems as an opportunity to outgrow his self-contempt and replace it with self-respect. It is hard for him to outgrow his childhood self-contempt in a social vacuum. He needs a self-respecting listener to set an example of moderation and self-acceptance for him to follow. Herman was finally able to admit his anger at God for taking his first wife, Marsha, after only three years of marriage. His anger at this loss was below the level of conscious awareness, but it was ruining his relationship with his new wife, Inga. She is in tears half the time.

After Herman's pent-up anger has been properly identified, expressed and drained, he is in a position to take some positive action in the real world. He has a power now that he did not have before -- the power of choice. He can write an anger letter to God. He can even accept his own contribution to Inga's distress as a human imperfection on his part and not as a crime to feel guilty about. He can choose to assume appropriate responsibility for rectifying the situation by apologizing to Inga for sniping at her for every least little thing. He can also choose to catch himself in the act of doing it and decide to stop. He can get closure now and feel relief from his unfinished business.

Vignette: I Can't Feel My Life.

Eva felt numbed out. She didn't know how she felt and she didn't care how she felt. She didn't even care whether she knew how she felt. She didn't care about anything -- her job, her family, her friends or herself. She didn't feel like living. She felt like "quitting" by committing suicide. But she couldn't do that, either. She didn't even care about dying.

Eva's Early Recollection #1: "I was very sick when I was seven. I had an operation. My parents would come and visit me. My mother would try to comfort me, but all she could do was cry. My father got upset with her crying. He would wait out in the hall till she was ready to go home."

Facet Analysis

1. "I have no one to comfort me. I have to comfort myself."

2. "I don't want to be weak like my mother. My father despises her weakness and so do I."

3. "Crying doesn't help. It only makes things worse."

4. "I want to be strong like my father. That way, nothing can hurt me."

Eva's Early Recollection #2: "After my operation, my mother and father fought, but they never kissed and made up any more. He was mean to her, like he didn't care about her. He called her "stupid." He would slam the door and leave. She would cry for a long time. I was scared he wouldn't come back."

Facet Analysis

1. "Weak people, like my mother (and me), can be abandoned at any time."

2. "It doesn't pay to be weak and to care about someone."

3. "Someone can hurt you terribly just by leaving. I won't let myself care about anyone that much."

4. "Women are out of control. They can be victimized by someone strong."

5. "Anger is painful and scary. It doesn't pay to get angry."

Eva used her numbing out as her way of preventing terrible things from happening to her. She thought she was "controlling" her emotions. She did not know any other example of control to follow, so she made up her own. It has cost her dearly. She has no close friends. She cannot feel her life.

She, too, thought she was being "strong." She did not know the difference between strength and phony strongness. She kept wondering, "If I am so strong, why can't I solve my problems?" She is now learning how to correct these two very basic mistakes.

Eva is replacing these "solutions" with more appropriate ones. She is learning to control her anger by expressing it appropriately. When her co-worker took credit for a project she had worked on for a week, she said, *"It makes me angry when you do that, Ralph."* It took courage, but she did it. She overcame her scary fears of abandonment, displeasing, weakness and all the other facets of her self-contempt. In that moment, she felt like she was coming out of a shell, a shell she didn't know she was in. She had managed her emotions like an adult. She had taken the first step toward an identity as a three-dimensional, warm-blooded, grown-up human being.

#53. THE ONE-TWO PUNCH

Now that we have told Ralph the truth about our anger, what do you suppose will happen? Will he kiss us on the cheek? Will he say, "Thank you for calling this to my attention?"

Certainly not. He will probably lash back with something to throw us off balance, to exonerate himself at our expense, such as:

"That's your problem."

"You're always angry."

"Who cares if you're angry?"

"You are too sensitive."

"You're crazy."

. . .and so on.

This is his way of solving the problem that we have just created for him. He does not know how to solve anger problems, so he tries to invalidate the whole thing out of existence. That way, he won't have to solve it. We call these comeback responses "deflections."

1. Our first step is to identify these rejoinders as mischief. They do not need to be said, but Ralph doesn't know what else to say. He hasn't had the course.

2. We do not take the rejoinder at face value as if it made sense. We do not say, "I am not always angry." That is walking into his trap. We have just been diverted from our anger path onto a dead-end street. Ralph wins and we lose.

3. We do not take these remarks as if they were a reflection on our anger or on us. Ralph is only firing for effect, to get us off his case. His hurtful response has nothing to do with our worth as a person. We are worthwhile no matter what comes out of his mouth.

4. Ralph feels inadequate to cope with our anger. He is seeking to relieve the pain of his own inadequacy by tearing us and our anger down. We do not have to let him get away with it. He wouldn't really feel any better if we did. Nothing would be gained; we would both lose.

5. We can now ask ourselves, *"How has this mischief made me feel?"* The answer will come out: angry.

6. Having identified these anger deflections as mere mischief, we can now go on to do the unexpected. We can tell the truth for a second time: *"You have just made it worse, Buster. I am angrier now than I was before."* That is the truth. That is the issue we need to be dealing with, not his nonsensical, phony deflections.

7. This technique is called the "One-Two Punch." After we have hit him with our anger in the first place, we are prepared in advance for his snappy comeback with a backup punch.

8. Ralph will be surprised by our resoluteness, competence and our preparedness in these anger matters. He may even come to respect us and apologize for making us angry in the first place.

9. He may try to deflect our one-two punch with another jab of his own. "Where did you get that stuff? Did you read it in a book somewhere?" That will make us angry too, but we are prepared for it. *"You just did it again. You're making it worse."* In so saying, we are letting him know that we have no intention of letting these deflections throw us off course. These people do not usually get past the first backup punch, but we are ready for them if they try.

#54. PATIENCE

Some of us want our own way and we want it now. We do not see why life does not give it to us. That makes us angry. Our impatience has many facets:

"Life Is supposed to give me what I want -- my mother always did."

"If I don't get what I want, I won't know who I am."

"I can't wait. Waiting is a waste of time, and waste makes me feel like I am irresponsible, guilty and out of control."

The antidote to our impatience is patience. If we can put our wants in a more moderate, mature perspective, we are more likely to get them. Not only that, but we will live longer and enjoy the wait a lot more. We can tell ourselves that we do not have to take the disappointment or delay personally. We are worthwhile human beings in spite of it in the meantime.

#55. PEELING YOUR ANGER ARTICHOKE

As you have already seen, people can learn to use a focusing question to pry off the upper layers of their emotional response and get at the fundamental issues which have been overlooked and neglected. We can learn to stop seeing anger as if it were an unstoppable flow of molten lava and choose instead to see it as an artichoke that can be peeled down with the right utensils and put to constructive, instead of destructive, use.

To peel back the layers of our loved one's anger, we begin with the focusing question such as, *"Who are you angry at?"* This question focuses their attention on the here and now and gives them permission to be angry. It expresses an intelligent, sincere concern on our part for our friend or loved one in spite of this unpleasant situation. It demonstrates that we are prepared, in control and competent. These qualities are very reassuring in any crisis.

For example, our friend Sara may be angry about her job. We can ask, *"What happened to make you so angry?"*

"Sheila told the boss I was in the cafeteria when I was really down on the fourth floor trying to trace an order that she had lost."

"Who are you angry at?"

"At Sheila!"

"What angers you the most at Sheila?"

"Here I am, trying to save her bacon and she rats on me to the boss, Judy, who just loves to stick it to me. She knows that I should have gotten that promotion instead of her."

"That sounds like you are angry at being victimized."

"Darn right."

"What angers you the most?"

"That I was trying to help her out and she didn't appreciate it. Judy didn't appreciate it, either. She thought I was lying."

"You felt that your goodness was all for nothing. What angers you the most?"

"It's so unfair. I was doing her a favor and she stabbed me in the back."

"You are angry at this betrayal. Sheila and Judy both betrayed you. You are the victim of this unfairness. Who else are you angry at?"

"I'm more angry at Judy. She has responsibilities. She should know how to manage people better than that."

"You are angry at her irresponsibility. What else angers you?"

"That there's nothing I can do about it."

"Now you are angry at feeling powerless and out of control."

"I didn't realize that my anger was so complicated."

"We're only halfway through. Who else are you angry at besides Sheila and Judy?"

"There isn't anyone else. Wait, I'm angry at myself, for knocking myself out all this time."

"What angers you the most about yourself?"

"It's that I must be stupid or something. I never learn. I'll probably do it again tomorrow. I'm such a pushover, and it's my fault."

The Good for Nothing Syndrome

"Sara, when your goodness doesn't pay off fairly, you feel good for nothing, stupid and worthless. You are angry at yourself for letting it happen and for failing to prevent it."

"It's the story of my life. I remember taking my little brother to the park. When we got home, my mom bawled me out for not telling her where we went. I really got clobbered."

"She didn't appreciate your consideration, did she? This is a recollection of feeling good for nothing, stupid and irresponsible in spite of your good intentions. Now, when something similar happens in the present that reminds you of this pain from the past, you feel that your childhood 'worthlessness' has been confirmed."

"Hasn't it?"

"No. You were not worthless then and you are not worthless now. You were an imperfect little girl doing what you thought was right. You meant well -- it just didn't turn out that way."

"I keep setting myself up for it. That's stupid."

"There is another explanation that has nothing to do with native intelligence. You are not doing this consciously or rationally. You are a good person and you try to do the right thing. There are times when people cannot appreciate what you do because they have negative feelings about themselves which prevent them from appreciating you or anyone else."

"That's right. They don't pat anybody on the back. It would kill them."

"Moreover, you are consistently behaving in ways that maintain and confirm the roles that you carried over from childhood into adulthood. It is not your fault that you do."

"I'm consistent all right. How can I stop?"

"By replacing your role as 'The Good for Nothing Child' with an adult identity of your own. It is called self-respect."

"I've never had a lot of that, I'll tell you. How do I get in on it?"

"By earning it, through doing homework."

"What is that?"

"Very often, it takes the form of doing the unexpected on your own terms instead of reacting to someone elses. Tell me, what does Judy expect you to do about your anger at her?"

"She expects me to swallow it. That's what I've always done."

"That's another role that you play, the 'Pleasing Child' who can never get angry."

"That's true. I never get angry."

"Yes, you do. You just aren't aware of it and you don't show it. You suppress it and you never let anyone know it's down there, not even yourself."

"That sounds like me."

Homework

"Now that you know what Judy expects, you can choose not to do it and do something else instead. What is the last thing Judy and Sheila expect you to do?"

"I don't know."

"The last thing they expect you to do is to tell the truth. To say, 'I'm very angry about what happened yesterday. I just want you to know how angry I am.'"

"I couldn't do that."

"Why not?"

"It's too scary."

"What scares you the most?'"

"They wouldn't like me."

"They don't like you now. You are just their victim."

"You're right."

"What's the worst thing that could happen?"

"Come to think of it, which I never did before, nothing would happen."

"They wouldn't send you to your room, would they? They are not your mother, and you are not six years old. Can you say that to them tomorrow?"

"I'm still not sure."

"It's still scary, isn't it? It will be scary until after you have done it. What is it called when you overcome your scary fears from childhood?"

"Fearlessness?"

"No. You are not fearless, you are afraid. It's called courage. If you have no fears, you don't need courage."

"That's what I need. How do I get it?"

"Courage is the willingness to take a risk. You don't wait until you get it, you go ahead and do it anyway."

"That's not easy."

"Children do what is easy, grown-ups do what is difficult."

"I'll do it."

"Good. Afterwards, you will have feelings of accomplishment, success and the confidence that you can do it again."

"Sounds good to me. It's worth the risk. I have really learned a lot about myself from all these questions. They make me think about things I've never thought about before."

"You knew the answers. You just didn't know that you knew them. We have used these focusing questions to make your unconscious fears and attitudes conscious. Now you can put your childhood carryovers into an adult perspective. You can see things more clearly now.

"That's how I feel -- like I've been liberated from something that's been holding me back."

"Liberated from what?"

"From the me I used to be."

"And what has taken its place?"

"A feeling that I have an identity of my own. I can make my own choices now."

"That feeling is called self-respect."

#56. PHYSICAL EXERTION

Running around the block, punching a pillow, chopping wood, hollering down a rain barrel and throwing a rubber brick at the television set are all tried and true techniques for releasing the pain of your pent-up anger. Sometimes these activities release the energy generated by your adrenal glands as a physiological response to the provocation that made you angry. Your body prepared you for fight or flight. You did not do either one, but the energy is still down there looking for a place to go. For some people, working it off physically, one way or another, is a good third choice.

However, many people mistakenly believe that once the pent-up energy is worked off, the anger problem has been solved. They do not feel so frustrated because they have relieved the "powerlessness" component of their distress. They had the power of choice and they chose to pound their pillow or run around the block.

The anger component of their frustration, however, has not been relieved. It has not gone anywhere. That is why we recommend that after your workout, you identify the object of your anger, the nature of your grievance and sort it out as you have learned to do in these pages.

"For he who gives no fuel to fire puts it out, and likewise he who does not in the beginning nurse his wrath and does not puff himself up with anger takes precautions against it and destroys it."

- Plutarch

#57. PHYSICAL VENTILATION

It has long been known that ventilating anger directly can produce a cathartic release of pent-up emotions. A popular belief in both public and professional circles is that aggression is the instinctive catharsis for anger. Numerous metaphors can be found within our culture that capture the essence of how anger is to be released: "letting go," "blowing off steam," "getting rid of" and "letting it all hang out" are prime examples. This widespread belief that if people can be convinced, assisted or allowed to express their true feelings, they will benefit from it is a central component in almost all historically accepted therapeutic schools of thought. Psychotherapy is rooted in the prevalent belief that to discharge one's pent-up feelings and emotions is beneficial and cathartic. Furthermore, the psychiatrist John R. Marshall believes that "this conviction exists at all levels of psychological sophistication."

Contemporary "ventilationists" view the expression of anger, within the individual's social context and with regard to identifiable consequences, as an essential component in the healing process. Ventilationist theories concentrate on what the individual needs to accomplish to lower the level of angry arousal, reduce tension and eliminate anxiety. They maintain that aggressive actions will lower the level of angry arousal faster than any other method and that the aggressive release of emotions will prevent angry energy from causing internal damage. Numerous studies have proven this hypothesis to be correct. Cathartic aggression will lower a subject's blood pressure to an initial baseline state. The public health significance of this concept is further underlined in the epidemic proportion of fatalities in our nation due to heart disease, cancer, substance abuse and suicide.

Alexander Lowen's bioenergetics recommend the utilization of any type of aggressive anger release: shouting, screaming, howling, punching, kicking, slapping or biting -- anything short of physical assault and battery. It is commonly accepted that there is emotional value in the physical acts of throwing, hitting or breaking objects. Sports and other strenuous physical activities are lauded as socially accepted means of stress management and hostility. Catharsis is commonly understood to mean emotional release and the emptying of a physiological energy reservoir. Ventilating anger through the utilization of psychological relaxation techniques can be cathartic, but only when it restores a sense of control, reducing both the intrinsic rush of adrenaline that accompanies an unfamiliar and threatening situation and reducing the belief that one is powerless or helpless. Aggressive ventilation gets us in touch with underlying feelings, and the manner in which we choose to express anger directly affects how we feel. Experiences of emotional release feel very good and have therapeutic significance.

Those who want to let go of their anger need to rearrange their thought patterns, not just lower their pulse rate. Therapies that rely primarily on emotional release such as bioenergetics, primal scream, etc. frequently have precisely the opposite effect of catharsis, for instead of exorcising the anger, they can inflame it. The major side effect of the ventilationist approach has been to raise the general noise level of our lives, not to lessen our problems. Some therapists believe that people who are most prone to give vent to their rages get angrier, not less angry.

Hokanson has postulated the belief that aggressive catharsis is a learned reaction to anger and not an instinctive response. Cultural and generational differences exist in the desirability and normalcy of physical ventilation methods. Though boundaries exist, the common goal is for the anger to dissipate. Whatever works to relieve pent-up anger will bring catharsis because it removes the threat of violent rage and produces a calming sense of relaxation. The standards of angry behavior are individual, as are the anger-reducing behaviors which each individual employs. Regardless of individual makeup, the expression of anger is not the same as acting aggressively.

The prototype of physical ventilation can be witnessed in a child's tempter tantrum. All children will on occasion feel angry, frustrated, spiteful, resentful or unhappy and they will learn, through trial and error, what forms of emotional expression are socially appropriate and tolerated. Carol Tavris states that the first proto-emotion to emerge in babies is fear of loss, of the unfamiliar, of abandonment and of strangers. As a child's mental faculties develop, they identify the feeling of anger and realize that it has an effect. A child's anger has a socially significant purpose from the start. In a child's tantrum we can identify the key components of physical ventilation: screaming, crying, banging and kicking. A difference observed in adults is in the verbal components of cursing, taunting or pleading. Anger is formed, maintained and inflamed by the provocative statements made to ourselves and others.

In working out feelings of anger, our retaliation must be directed at the source of anger -- the person who made us angry or at someone who we believe deserves the blame. In the comfort and safety of a controlled environment, the visualized object of anger should receive exactly what he or she deserve. The utilization of plastic bats and punching bags has further amplified the physical potential of this technique. For those willing to take the risk and push themselves physically, this method can be lifesaving.

#58. POWER OF CHOICE

We all know what frustration feels like, don't we? But we do not know what the word frustration means. Frustration can be defined as feeling angry plus out of control. Our anger compounds when we feel powerless to do anything about our powerlessness! We are angry at ourselves for our inadequacy to solve the problem and relieve our pain.

The specific antidote to our feeling of powerlessness is the feeling that we are not powerless. There are some powers that we forgot we had. It is true that we cannot make our favorite TV star return our phone calls, but we are not totally out of control. There are other choices open to us. We can choose to call someone closer to home, to watch a different TV show or to use our judgment and solve our frustrating problem on a mature, creative basis. There is no law that says we cannot live our lives until we solve our frustrating problem perfectly. We can even choose to let go of it and do something else. Very often, the solution to the problem bubbles up after we have stopped trying so hard. The technique, then, is to give ourselves a choice that we forgot we had and see what happens.

#59. PREPARE IN ADVANCE, OR
"THE FRONT STOOP TECHNIQUE"

You know what is waiting for you when you get home or to your in-law's place. You can choose to barge right through that front door into a replay of the Crimean War or you can choose to do something different for the first time in your life.

For instance, you can choose to catch yourself about to go through that door and decide instead to stand for a minute on the front stoop and collect your thoughts.

Even though you have encountered this domestic barrage a thousand times before, you are always caught by surprise. You will find yourself saying things that a moment's forethought might have prevented. Now, before the barrage begins, you have the luxury of reminding yourself that there is mischief ahead and that you can choose to disengage from it, that you are a worthwhile human being in spite of the issues that will be raised, and that you can give emotional first aid if the situation requires it, and it probably will.

You can, in addition, refresh your memory as to the techniques that are available to you: "What Difference Does This

Make," "Disengage From the Mischief," "Agree With It" or whatever approach you are most comfortable with.

Thus forearmed, you are much better prepared to cope constructively and effectively with the encounter that awaits you. You can remind yourself that you deserve to be happy and successful and that you can choose not to use this confrontation to bring about the unhappiness that "worthless" people deserve. You will be shifting gears in advance from the old, vulnerable you to the new, prepared you. "Good luck" favors the prepared.

#60. PUNISHMENT

The word "punishment" comes from the Latin word *poena,* which means "pain." When someone causes us a painful grievance, we feel entitled to inflict pain in return. We justify our behavior by calling it "punishment," the implication being that the experience will benefit the miscreant's character and improve their deportment in the future. This is an overcompensatory good intention and keeps us from feeling as guilty as we would otherwise.

When we punish children, we are teaching them that they are "wrong" or "guilty." They take their punishment personally, as a reflection on their worth as a person. They hold themselves worthless. They cannot respect people who are as "guilty" or "wrong" as they seem to be. With repeated punishment, children become convinced of their worthlessness and begin to behave accordingly. Their negative behavior is consistent with their self-contempt. They feel that they do not deserve to behave positively.

Badness is not always what it seems to be. When there are two children in a family, both cannot be first best. One or the other seeks a place in the family constellation as the "First Worst Child." This child is a magnet for punishment. The more punishment that they receive, the more they are confirmed in their unhappy role.

Roger is not really a bad child. When the "good" sibling goes to camp, Roger moves into the vacant role and behaves very well. When the "good child" returns, Roger reverts to his previous role as "First Worst."

Wise parents do not play one child against the other. They do not say to Roger, "Why can't you behave like your sister Shirley?" In a way, this is like ordering the child to continue playing the role of the bad child. We are, in effect, ordering the child to disobey us. The child obeys our order and disobeys. Punishment, like all good intentions, is counterproductive.

Self-respecting parents understand negative behavior as mischief. They do not take it personally and they do not overreact or underreact. They understand mischief in terms of its purpose: to gain negative attention, gain power and control, get revenge or withdraw in discouragement. The parent responds appropriately to the negative purposes and replaces them with more positive purposes. For instance, they can give the child a choice between two positive activities. The third choice, making mischief, is not one of the options.

This approach requires time, energy and creativity. Parents who do not respect themselves do not trust their judgment. They do not value their own resources and feel inadequately prepared for the task of parenting. They are angry at their child and at themselves. They solve their problems all at once. They punish the child as if it were the child's fault that they cannot cope. The solution to the problem is not to control our children into mindless conformity, as they do in some cultures, but to replace the parents' self-contempt with self-respect.

Self-respecting parents encourage all their children to respect themselves as worthwhile human beings in their own right. When Roger misbehaves, they institute a system of logical consequences. If Roger refuses to eat dinner, knowing that his indulgent parents will feed him from the refrigerator, they wise up. They disengage from his mischief and take away from him the power to control them. They set limits. They let him know that if he does not finish, there will be no snacks to assuage his hunger pangs later. They give him a choice: eat now or wait until breakfast. It is his responsibility, not theirs. They involve the child in the procedure so that he feels like an active participant, not a victim of his unreasonable, all-powerful parents.

If Roger chooses not to eat and tests their resolve, the parents must make good on their agreement regarding snacks. Roger's consequence will be his hunger until the next morning. The issue here is not nutrition or inflicting pain, but securing the child's cooperation in running the household on an appropriate basis. Allowing children to dictate the rules is not appropriate.

Another logical consequence of mischief is our anger. We can manage our child's behavior by saying, *"It makes me angry when you push your little sister down. "* That is a consequence that children can understand.

Adult Punishment

The punishment of adult offenders is notoriously inefficient and counterproductive. Some people, who are not too far gone in their self-contempt, respond positively to the imposition of fines and penalties. They are not a significant social problem.

People who suffer from extreme self-contempt, however, do not see punishment in the same perspective that others do. Their logic is upside down. They take pride in their negative accomplishments and seek confirmation of their role as "First Worst" in the family and in the community. Punishment proves that they "can take it," as if such things needed proving. People who feel inferior and inadequate inside need to prove to themselves and others that they are not weak, but strong. The more severe the punishment, the stronger they are seen to be. Self-respecting people are not deceived. We know the difference between strength and phony, overcompensatory "strongness."

These offenders make us angry. We try to make our punishments unemotional through the institution of an "impersonal," "unbiased" judicial system, but that is just a good intention that we have for ourselves. We wish to appear impartial and free of vindictiveness. We have yet to impose a system of logical consequences whereby a thief knows in advance that if they are caught, they will have to make financial restitution to those that they robbed. Under our present system of jurisprudence, they get to keep the money. We do not have a system of active remorse. Victim and victimizer are prevented from seeing each other as human beings.

Offenders are sent to a correctional institution where they are further dehumanized and robbed of the last vestiges of their self-respect. Their perception of themselves as worthless is confirmed, and when they return to the community, their behavior will be consistent with their enhanced self-contempt.

George Clemenceau once said that war was much too important to be left to the generals. We could as easily say:

1. The law is much too important to be left to the lawyers.

2. Justice is much too important to be left to the judiciary.

3. Correction is much too important to be left to the correctors.

#61. RATIONALITOSIS

Marvin deals with his anger by rationalizing it away: "Oh, I'm sure he didn't mean to kick me in the knee. It was an accident," or "I miss my stereo, set but the man who stole it must have needed it more than I did. I just hope he likes good music."

This is an abuse of one's rational thought processes and a flagrant misuse of the mental faculties that we were born with. Marvin does it not because he is stupid, but because that is how he solves his potentially dangerous anger problem. If he allowed himself to feel his legitimate anger, he might have to do something rash, like stand up for himself. However, if he can deny his anger out of existence by using his "higher mental capacities," he can prevent the scary things that happen to people who expose their secret anger for everyone else to see.

Everyone assumes he is rational. Sometimes, as in Marvin's case, there is no basis for that assumption, but we assume it anyway. The truth is that there are two kinds of people in the world -- those who are sane and rational and those who only imagine that they are. We need an absurd word to distinguish the pseudo-rational folks in group 2 from the sane people in group 1. Since there is no word in the English language at present that will discriminate between these two categories of mental functioning, we have decided to call the process whereby people diagnose their own sanity without a license "rationalitosis."

Marvin's rationalizing does not relieve his anger -- he only thinks it does. His anger is still there. It is accumulating and making him sick. Someday, he will reach a point where he cannot rationalize it away anymore.

Marvin's mistake is to think that any problem can be solved rationally if we just put our minds to it. Emotional problems, such as anger, grief and guilt, cannot be solved rationally. We are not

RATIONALITOSIS

objective about our subjective feelings. We have feelings about our feelings. We have attitudes and expectations that were formed in our childhood, and they cannot be reasoned away. It is irrational to believe that they can. Some problems must be solved subjectively, but the schools do not teach us how that is done.

If Marvin can learn to accept his anger as a legitimate part of his makeup, he can then go on to the next step of peeling it down into its many components so that it can be understood and relieved properly. That is rational.

#62. REDUCE IT TO ABSURDITY

Most of the things we argue about are trivial. That is because the subject of the argument is not the issue. The issue is something farther down in our psyche, such as "I want my way and you're not giving it to me." It is absurd to argue about issues that aren't even the issue. If you can find the absurdity in an argument, which is unpleasant for everyone, you can break the tension with laughter. We aren't laughing at the other person, only at the absurdity in which we find ourselves.

Sam and Janet were late for a doctor's appointment. Sam was barreling down the freeway while Janet was upbraiding him for taking so long at the gas station. "Let me out of this car, right now," she demanded. Sam said, "Wait 'til I get 'er up to 100 miles an hour." They both laughed. The absurd, useless argument over past imperfections became irrelevant.

#63. RIDING IT OUT

Under the stress of an anger attack, we feel compelled to do something even if it doesn't make sense and makes things worse. We are trying to forestall any accusation that we are slackers or cowards under fire. "What will the neighbors think if I just stand there like a dummy?"

"I can't feel my life. "

Carrie Fisher
Post Cards From The Edge
1987, Simon & Schuster, NY, NY

So we go into overdrive and say, "Don't be angry, you'll have a heart attack," or "Calm down, everything will be all right." Well, it won't. We are not dealing rationally with the real issue, which is that our loved one has a legitimate grievance and it needs to be addressed. We are doing something about their anger, but it isn't something that needs to be done. It is well intentioned mischief. Our unconscious motivations to look useful have nothing to do with coping effectively with a loved one's rage. They have nothing to do with solving problems in the real world. We are "solving" fictitious problems that do not need to be solved. We are escaping from our feelings of "copelessness" into mindless, counterproductive busyness.

When we feel inadequate to cope, we feel compelled to say such things as, "Stop that this instant" or "Don't you dare talk to me like that." We give ourselves the illusion of activity although we are doing nothing to make things better. We behave as if any activity were better than no activity at all. We feel as though we have to do something, we just don't know what. Maybe there is no such "have to."

The antidote to this absurd strategy becomes apparent immediately. The opposite of doing something is not doing something. It is a choice that we did not know we had. Twenty-five hundred years ago, the Buddha told his followers, "Don't just do something, stand there." This is difficult advice for activists like ourselves to take. We are impatient to put the problem behind us, but our counterproductive actions are like pouring kerosene on the flames, which only makes the problem worse.

We call this technique of doing nothing, which runs counter to our innermost strivings, "Riding It Out." Sometimes we can expedite the healing of an anger attack by listening and validating our loved one's grief simply by our unobtrusive presence. We may nod our head in sympathy, empathize with their distress, but we are not jumping up and down like a jack-in-the-box trying to relieve our feelings of inadequacy at the expense of their pain.

Sometimes our forebearance on these occasions allows other people to come up with an appropriate solution to the anger problem sooner than they would have otherwise. Their solution to this problem will be better for them than our well-intentioned but ill-advised intervention would ever be.

#64. SCAPEGOATS

When life makes us angry, we look for someone to take the burden of pain off our shoulders. When we feel burdened by guilt, we displace our painful emotion onto the head of someone who is powerless to do anything about it. When we are feeling both angry and guilty, we must find a scapegoat that we can use as an outlet for energies that threaten to blow us up from the inside.

In ancient times, superstitious, "backward" societies used to tie their griefs to the horns of a goat and throw it over a cliff. It made them feel a lot better.

During the dark ages, impoverished individuals would hire themselves out as "sin eaters," consuming food that held the "sins" of those preparing the food. Having taken on the wrongs of others, they would then be punished by the people.

In recent years, a modern technological society has been known to feel guilty and angry about losing a war and tied its anger and guilt around the neck of a helpless segment of its population. As a matter of national policy, it threw its own citizens into gas ovens. This "advanced" society, was also looking for fast relief from its collective pain in ways that did not work in the long run. This modern society had failed to evolve. Its veneer of civilization was very thin.

Looking for scapegoats is a syndrome. It is a combination of pathological attitudes that occur together. These attitudes may or may not be conscious, but they determine the scapegoater's behavior just the same. These attitudes were acquired in the past, but they are applied in the present where they do not conform with the demands of reality. They override reality for a short while and the pressure is relieved temporarily. However, reality has not been dealt with appropriately and the pressure will build up again. The individual will eventually blow up from inside.

These are some of the attitudinal components of the "Scapegoat Syndrome":

1. "I am not a victim anymore. My scapegoat is the victim now."

2. "I am the victimizer, which hurts a lot less."

3. "I am not powerless, for I have the power to victimize."

4. "I am not out of control. I am in control. I am making this victimization happen."

5. "I am not an inferior loser, I am a superior winner."

6. "I am not wrong, I am right."

7. "I am not worthless, my victim is worthless."

8. "My problem is not insoluble, for I have just solved it."

9. "I do not have to change and grow -- that is too scary. I can stay just the way I am forever."

10. "I am not responsible for my own downfall. Others are to blame. I am exempt from responsibility."

11. "I am angry and I need a safe outlet for my anger. This is it."

What do all of these attitudes have in common? They are all overcompensations for feelings of inferiority and inadequacy to cope. Overcompensation, in turn, is characteristic of people who feel inferior and hold themselves in contempt.

Gloria was the scapegoat in her family. Her father and the three boys were angry at their mother for her cruelty. They didn't dare confront her directly, so they dumped their anger on Gloria, who strongly resembled her. As it often happens, the scapegoat turned out to be the strongest member of the family. The other members of the family were enabled to maintain their sanity at her expense. She nearly cracked under the strain, but she did not.

Gloria needed support and encouragement after she emerged from the ordeal of her childhood. She did her homework. As she did what pleased her and disengaged from mischief, she overcame her fear of expressing her anger. In place of her role as the world's scapegoat, she experienced an identity of her own as a worthwhile human being in spite of her faults and imperfections.

The antidote to looking for a scapegoat is self-respect. Self-respecting people do not have to solve their emotional problems on the backs of people who had nothing to do with the case. They do not deny their contribution to their own distress and do not take their setbacks as a reflection of their worth as a person. They can accept their imperfection and learn from their mistakes. Each time they bounce back from a reversal on the basis of new information and insight, they grow as an individual and strengthen their self-respect. They feel competent to solve problems in ways that work.

Do's and Don'ts

If you seek out scapegoats and wish to outgrow this carryover from kindergarten, remember that you can be angry at what happened or at the individual who caused you this grievance. However, you need not be angry at yourself for being imperfect.

173

You can choose to accept your imperfection. You are worthwhile in spite of it. When you make this change in your attitude, your anger at yourself will be released. If this anger at yourself is not down there, it cannot blow you up from the inside. You will not have to release your anger at the expense of a fellow human being.

You can choose to respect yourself in spite of what happened. A mistake in judgment is not a crime, it's only a reflection of your human imperfection. You are not a criminal. You cannot build yourself up by tearing yourself down with self-criticisms or by tearing others down, either.

Catch yourself about to use your spouse, child or co-worker as a scapegoat and choose not to. Ask yourself a focusing question: *"Who am I really angry at? How can I express this anger in a way that will give me some relief?"*

If you are the scapegoat, catch yourself taking your current setback as if it were a victimization. Victims are "inferior" and "worthless." You cannot respect such people. You can only hold them in contempt. You can ask yourself, *"Am I perceiving victimization where no victimization is required in the real world? Is this mischief? If so, I can disengage from it."*

Catch yourself taking this negative situation personally, as a wipeout of your self-respect. You are not powerless and an out-of-control victim, for you have the power of choice. You can choose to perceive what happened as one of the ups and downs of life that occurs in an imperfect world. You can say, *"It makes me angry when you dump your problems on me."*

#65. SENSE OUT OF NONSENSE

When we are fighting, we often make the mistake of taking nonsense seriously and trying to make sense of it. "You're wrong." "No, you're wrong." This approach is not productive. We have to be smarter than that.

"Smarter" often means hearing the sense behind the nonsense. "You're wrong," often means, "I am angry at you for what you did." The issue is not rightness or the absence thereof, but the other person's anger. That being the case, it is smarter to address the real issue so that it can be resolved. *"You sound angry. What happened to make you so angry?"*

Vignette: I Have To Understand Myself

Carla overheard Jeff and Lorraine talking in the employees lounge. Lorraine was saying, "How can they fire Steve? I can't get my work done without him." Jeff was saying, "Never mind Steve. I'd worry about my own job if I were you." Lorraine got up and stormed out of the room. Carla felt bad for both of them. She does not like to see people unhappy. She was about to go into her old routine of calming Jeff down by explaining Lorraine's underlying motivation to him, so that the whole thing would make sense to him. She caught herself just in time. She realized that Jeff wasn't interested in sense or motivation. He had his own agenda and it did not include rational thought processes. She realized that she didn't understand Jeff's vulnerabilities well enough to explain anything to him. She also caught herself feeling responsible for solving other people's anger problems, which she had no real responsibility to do. Instead, she chose to let Jeff continue to think what he thinks. She didn't feel guilty, irresponsible or out of control. She had made an appropriate choice in her own head. No one knew about it but her, but it was an accomplishment just the same. She had let go of these old habits and roles that she used to play in grammar school and didn't need anymore. She saw how much nonsense there was in the world around her. She had no obligation at all to make sense of it for anyone but herself. She decided to lay her burden down. She felt relief, independence, security within herself and all the other facets of self-respect.

"I am not required to finish the task; neither am I permitted to put it down."

Hillel

#66. SHOULDING

We expect people to do what they should do and we become very angry at them when they do not. We attempt to relieve our anger by reminding them that they did not do what they should have done and that they should do it in the future. This process is called "Shoulding." It is another example of a mindless good intention. It does not work because we neglected to determine the offender's purpose in not doing what should have been done.

Maybe they did not do it because they knew you would erupt like a volcano if they didn't. Well, you just confirmed their expectations. They are making mischief and you are paying off. Telling them what they "should" do is irrelevant to their underlying purposes, which is to get your goat. They have the power to do it and you have given it to them.

Like all good intentions, "shoulding" is self-indulgent. Its true purpose is not to improve the offender's behavior in the future, but to make ourselves feel morally superior to folks who do not do what they should. This is our way of overcompensating for our own feelings of inferiority. Our anger at the other person has a note of moral indignation and righteousness which is hard to refute. It makes communication between equal members of the human race impossible.

Shoulding is also counterproductive. People resent our superior airs and the implication that they are too stupid to know what they should have done or too lazy to do it. This, too, precludes cooperative problem solving.

What does "should" mean? "Should" is merely a preference. Children should pick up their toys so we do not step on them. It is a preference, not a moral crime when they fail to do so. They are not guilty, merely imperfect. It is our responsibility to bring about the desired or preferred behavior by securing positive cooperation instead of negative rebellion.

Vignette: You Should Walk the Dog

Marcy loved her dog -- she just didn't love to walk it. Her mother kept telling her that she should walk the dog. Marcy already knew that she should; that was not the problem. The problem was that she didn't want to. Her mother's nagging did not succeed in making her want to.

Marcy was 18 years old. She wanted all the advantages of adulthood while retaining all of her exemptions from childhood. She was on the cusp of growing up. She wanted it both ways. She didn't see why she shouldn't have what she wanted.

Her mother learned to stop nagging Marcy about the dog. When Marcy next said, "I don't want to," her mother was ready for her. She used our technique of "agreeing with it." She said, *"I know you don't want to. Do we only do what we want? Grown-ups do what is required. Even if you don't want to, do it anyway."*

Mother didn't get into a power struggle over the time of the dog walking. Marcy could choose when to do it. If she didn't do it, there would be a logical consequence -- the dog would have to stay at her married sister's house for a week.

Marcy chose to do what reality requires dog owners to do. She saw it as a growth opportunity. She assumed responsibility for her pet and for herself. She felt that she had made a mature decision in her own behalf. She was outgrowing her childhood exemptions and replacing them with something better, self-respect.

Do's and Don't's

Do not stand in moral judgment on people who fail to do what they should do. They are not "wrong," merely imperfect. You are no more perfect than they are.

You have the right to your preference, and so does the other person. Perhaps you need to find out what those preferences are so that you can work out a compromise. Do not assume that their preferences are invalid and inferior to your own.

Use logical consequences to shape behavior in the desired direction. Do not protect people from the consequences of their irresponsibility. Let them experience the negative aftereffects. Do not reward them by putting on an emotional fireworks display for them.

When people "should" on you, do not take it personally. You are a worthwhile human being in spite of what did or did not happen. Your worth as a person is not the issue. Do not make it the issue. You might ask yourself what your purpose was in not doing what should have been done. Did reality prevent you from doing it or did you have purposes of your own? Were these purposes positive or negative? If they were negative, then you were just making mischief. Mischief making is a preference, it just isn't a very constructive preference. Do not be surprised if the outcome is negative.

#67. THE SILENT TREATMENT

The "Silent Treatment" is not to be confused with the technique of "Riding It Out" or "Admirable Restraint." This technique, unlike the others, is not appropriate for the reality of the situation. The "Silent Treatment" is immature, inappropriate and counterproductive. It is not positive communication, but negative communication. Herman's silence is sending Florence a message, "I won't talk and you can't make me." Florence is getting it loud and clear.

When Herman gets angry, he goes into his "control" mode. He shuts down and clams up. Florence used to pound on his chest, "Speak to me, Herman." His lips were sealed. He was a fortress under siege. He would not crack.

In the second grade, we used to call this "sulking and pouting." Over the age of twelve, it is called the "Silent Treatment" or the Big ST, as we call it for short in the anger biz.

Herman has found that he cannot control very much in this world, but he sure can control his lips. As a kid, he could hold his breath until he turned blue. His mother caved in every time. Now it is Florence who is under his power, pleading for mercy, putty in his hands.

At the same time that he is accomplishing his power and control purpose, he is also punishing her for offending him. He is getting revenge on her in a way that leaves no scars. If she were to complain about his immature anger management technique, he can say, in all innocence, "What did I do? I didn't say anything!" Maybe that is the problem. Maybe he should have said something.

Florence has learned to take away from Herman the power to drive her nuts with his mischief. She knows now that her life will go on whether this bozo talks to her or not. She can now say, *"Could it be that you will talk to me when you are good and ready? That's all right, I'm going to the movies. Maybe we can have a chat when I come back. Or not."*

She can also choose to tell Herman the truth about herself: *"It hurts me when you clam up like that. If you continue to hurt me like this, there may be a consequence that you will not care for. It is entirely up to you."* This technique is called "Giving Him a Choice."

THE SILENT TREATMENT

#68. SOMATIZATION

We all know what happens when Uncle Harry gets angry. His face turns beet red, his eyes pop out, the vein in his forehead starts throbbing, he stutters and sputters -- that is somatization. His anger is manifesting itself somatically, that is, physically. "Soma" means "body," and our anger affects our body more than we realize.

When we become angry, our body prepares itself for a crisis. We prepare for fight or flight. Our adrenal glands start to secrete energy-giving adrenalin, our digestive system shuts down and our heart pumps faster in order to get blood into the extremities where it is needed. We are all afraid that Uncle Harry is going to have a cardiovascular accident someday if he doesn't calm down. We used to call these accidents "apoplectic strokes," which heightened the association between the somatic event and the strong emotion that precipitated it.

Heart researchers at Duke University recently discovered that it isn't only the erupting volcanoes like our uncle who die of anger-related physical disorders. People who silently fume over their grievances are doing themselves in as well. In fact, they are now saying that mismanaged anger ranks with cigarette smoking, obesity and high-fat diets as a major factor in fatal heart disease. They found from standardized tests that women who showed signs of suppressed anger were three times more likely to die over the 18-year study period as women who did not show high anger levels.

Another study with lawyers showed that only 4% of the easygoing subjects died by the age of 50, but those who ranked in the upper 25% of the hostility chart suffered a mortality rate five times as high; one in five subjects died. In 1988, almost one hundred thousand Americans died of cardiovascular diseases. How many of them might have been saved by teaching them how to express their anger in the middle ground between erupting and suppressing?

Researchers have found that college students with high anger scores tended to have elevated levels of low-density lipoprotein, the "bad" cholesterol, and abnormally low levels of high-density lipoprotein, the "good" cholesterol. This imbalance increases the risk of cardiovascular disease in later years. The arteries grow stiffer, the heart muscle weakens, the liver and kidney are damaged and too much fat is released into the bloodstream. The system cannot tolerate this internal abuse, a weak spot ruptures and the individual suffers the consequences of fifty years of mismanaged anger. Death from a heart attack is the ultimate somatization.

Dr. Bernie Siegel writes about the effect of the mind on human physiology. As a cancer doctor, he sees malignancy as "partly a reaction to a set of circumstances that weaken the body's defenses." He describes two kinds of depressed patients -- those who give up and withdraw from normal activity and those who "continue with their routines" and put on a "show of happiness, when on the inside their lives have come to lack all meaning."

Both types of depressed patients have one thing in common: They are both mismanaging their anger. They are keeping that energy inside instead of letting it out in appropriate, healthy ways. In most cases of depression, the individuals are angry at themselves and they do not even know it. They do not feel angry, for their anger has turned to depression.

Dr. Siegel describes a typical cancer patient as experiencing "a lack of closeness to his parents" (abandonment); "a lack of the kind of unconditional love ("I am unlovable") that could have assured him of his intrinsic value" ("I am worthless") and an "ability to overcome challenges" ("I feel inadequate to cope"). Such a person tends to view himself as stupid, clumsy, weak and inept despite real achievements that are often the envy of classmates ("Whatever I do, it isn't good enough").

These aspects of the typical cancer patient are all facets of self-contempt. When we have the twin determinants of mismanaged anger at the self in a context of self-contempt, it places the organism under severe stress. We can see how this stress would, after many years, result in a breakdown of the body's defenses. The resulting malignancy is, in a way, an outcome of the individual's lifelong, self-destructiveness which arises out of the conviction that "worthless" people do not deserve to live and be happy -- they only deserve to suffer and die.

Do's and Don'ts:

Do not live on other people's terms. Live on your own terms as a worthwhile human being in spite of your faults and imperfections.

Do not live in fear of displeasing other people -- that is dependency. Do what pleases you for a change.

Do not store up your anger until you explode. Express your anger appropriately at the time.

If you cannot tell the person you are angry at that you are angry, tell someone else that you can trust.

Do not use euphemisms for your anger. You are not "bothered" or "upset," you are angry.

If you cannot express your anger orally, write it down in the form of an anger letter or draw an anger picture.

Do not suppress your anger for fear of being called "weak." Emotions are not a weakness; we are not made of stone. Emotions are a legitimate part of the human condition and they need to be managed constructively.

"Do we only do what is easy? Children do what is easy; grown-ups do what is difficult. "

Rudolph Dreikurs

Do not let your anger control you. You must control it in positive ways. Your anger has no brains, you do.

It takes courage to overcome the fears of a lifetime. Courage is the willingness to take a risk. After we take the risk, we often find that it wasn't so scary after all.

You are angrier at yourself than you realize. Write yourself an anger letter. You may not feel angry, but your anger is down there below the level of conscious awareness. Sometimes it helps to just start writing a letter to yourself about some of your childhood "sins" of omission and commission. Not only do you feel "guilty," but you are angry at yourself for "allowing" these things to happen -- as if you could have prevented them. Once you start writing in this frame of mind, a process of association begins and one thing leads to another. Get it all out. If you get tired, you can stop for today and write some more tomorrow. You do not have to do it perfectly; it will be good enough as it is.

#69. SORT OUT THE ANGER MISCHIEF
FROM THE NONMISCHIEF

When people get angry, they often do things that do not need to be done, like yelling, screaming, cursing, hitting, abusing, threatening, stabbing, shooting and so on. Some of this mischief can be very scary indeed. With practice, serious students of anger management can learn to disengage emotionally from this useless flak so that they can intervene appropriately and effectively. This does not mean that they are "ignoring" the mischief. Not at all. They know exactly what is going on and they are choosing to focus their efforts on the kernel of legitimate anger that triggered this anger attack in the first place. They know that there is a grievance down there somewhere. It is their task to cut through the barrage of mischief and get to the real issue so they can put it in perspective and relieve it. They can say, *"You must be very angry. What happened to make you so angry?"* (see #55, Peeling Your Anger Artichoke).

#70. SPANKING

Parents have been spanking kids since time began. Here again, there are two ways of doing it -- the right way and the wrong way.

The wrong ways:

1. Spanking a child as a release for your pent-up anger.

2. Spanking a child indiscriminately for no reason.

3. Waiting for father to come home six hours after the fact.

4. "Pounding sense" into a child for his or her own good.

We must not victimize our children for our own unhealthy purposes. Children have a way of paying us back when they are six feet tall. One way they have of repaying us is to brutalize our grandchildren. Another way is to self-destruct. That will teach us a lesson we will never forget.

We define spanking as a swat on the behind. Spanking a child in order to set limits on out-of-control behavior is the right way. Giving a choice between behaving and misbehaving, with its consequent spanking, is the right way. If the child tests us to see if we mean it, we must not flunk the test.

"Spanking" should be a logical consequence of the child's own behavior. If we are angry at what happened, we are not going to think in terms of logical consequences. We need to manage our own anger before we make this decision to intervene negatively in our child's life. We want to teach them the right lessons, not the wrong ones.

"I wouldn't belong to any country club that would have me for a member."

Groucho Marx

When we are illogical and punitive, we teach our children that people are unreasonable and unpredictable. They cannot trust such people and they have no effective defense against them. We cannot improve their behavior by betraying their trust.

When we give our SusieBelle a swat for running out into the street, she gets the connection between her behavior and the consequence. We are not victimizing her or making her feel worthless. We just want to change the behavior, not destroy her self-respect. If we tear down her self-respect, she will hold herself in contempt and behave accordingly. We will find ourselves doing more spanking than we had planned to do.

#71. STAY ANGRY

After a few seconds or minutes, anger can begin to transmute into unhealthy by-products such as depression, anxiety, obsessing, paranoia, eating disorders, suicidal impulses, substance abuse, etc. We are then stuck with these by-products, for we have lost sight of the anger that we had ten minutes before. This "Stay Angry" technique reminds us that our original anger was a healthy, legitimate emotion. If we can stay angry and manage it properly, before it goes sour, we can spare ourselves the pain of these self-destructive derivatives. We can choose to stay angry until our anger dissipates, as healthy anger does after a short while. Then you don't have to stay angry anymore.

#72. STRESS

Stress is a consequence of exceeding our ability to adapt. We try to do too much too soon. We try to go higher, farther and faster while sitting in our office or raising our child. There are two obvious ways of relieving stress. Pretending it is not there is not one of them.

1. We can manage our external environment so that it does not exceed our ability to adapt to it. For example, we can play eighteen holes of golf instead of thirty-six.

2.   We can improve our ability to adapt to the experiences of everyday life.   We can start by identifying the attitudes and convictions from childhood that are still impeding our competence to cope and to get rid of them.   We can get out of our own way.

"Stress" was invented in 1946 by Dr. Hans Selye at McGill University in Montreal, Canada.   Before that we did not have stress, we had aggravation.   Aggravation was a much more descriptive word than the current terminology, which is more clinical and sterile.   Aggravation means weightiness or heaviness. It also implies an anger at having this weightiness on our backs or in our stomachs.   It connotes a grinding and gnawing that eats us up alive.   The new nomenclature is more attractive and it protects us from unpleasant, earthy associations.   Stress is high tech while aggravation is low tech.

Stress is seen as arising out of frustration, which is defined as anger plus powerlessness to do anything about it.   This fits our definition of stress as exceeding our ability to adapt and to solve adaptation problems.   When we are angry, we have a problem. When we do not know how to solve our anger problem because anger is unacceptable, our original problem compounds.   When we take our "failure" to solve our anger problem as a reflection on our worth as a person, then our original anger problem is compounded still further.

When we feel inadequate to cope, an insoluble problem acutely confirms our underlying feelings of copelessness and inferiority.   The original issue is no longer the issue that is killing us; it is this painful confirmation of our personal worthlessness as a human being.   This is a paradigm of aggravation.   It is very stressful.

These are some of the personal vulnerabilities that predispose us to being more stressed by life than we need to be. They are internal stressors.   We try to fight these stresses in the wrong way by overcompensating for them. We do too much in order to prove that we are not "weak," "little" or "stupid" any more. These overcompensatory solutions work in reverse. They make things worse and the negative outcome proves that we were right the first time, we are as useless and inferior as we felt ourselves to be. That is stress.

Do's and Don'ts

Catch yourself trying to prove that you are not worthless. It is a fictitious problem and it does not have to be solved. Your antidote to feeling worthless is not to climb mountains, but to accept yourself as a worthwhile human being in spite of your faults and imperfections.

Catch yourself trying to adapt perfectly. That is the ultimate overcompensation, and you cannot do it. It is a set-up for failure. You are not required to adapt perfectly. You are required to adapt well enough, and that does not require any "proving" or "demonstrating" at all. You will accomplish a lot more with a lot less stress if you can manage to put these extreme attitudes from childhood into a more mature, appropriate perspective. Your stress level will come down considerably and so will your blood pressure.

Do not fight the stress, for fighting the stress will only make it worse. At the other extreme, do not go along with stress in order to find out how much of a beating you can take before your heart explodes -- in finding out, it may be too late. In Japan, they call it *karoshi* or death by overwork.

Ask yourself, *"What am I trying to prove and to whom? Who cares? Can it be proven? Does it work? Can I choose to stop overcompensating? Can I let it go? How good is good enough?"* The answer is, *"As good as I am right now, that is good enough. I will be a lot better if I can let go of these bad habits from third grade. In the meantime, I am good enough as I am."*

Replace your feelings of inferiority with feelings of adequacy and competency by giving yourself some simple homework to do. For instance, if you are too busy to think about making your spouse happy right now, do not put it off until you retire. Make it happen today, of your own free will and volition. Or catch yourself having impossibly high standards for your child or your co-worker and feeling anger at their failure to live up to your expectations. You can choose to let your expectations go. You will feel relief from your anger and from the excessive, inappropriate responsibility you have been assuming for a fellow human being. The next homework would be to do the same thing for yourself -- to accept yourself as worthwhile right now, as you are in the present, not as you will be in the future after you accomplish some external goal. On the basis of realistic self-acceptance, you will live to accomplish more goals in the long run and you will enjoy them more.

A major source of stress comes from trying to control in negative ways what we learned in childhood. You can catch yourself controlling in order to prevent disasters in the future. Choose instead to live in the present and do what reality requires you to do, no more and no less. If you take care of the present in a mature, appropriate way, your future will have fewer disasters than the other way around.

#73. SUBSTANCE ABUSE

We do not usually relate alcoholism, drug addiction and chemical dependency to anger, but there is often an anger component in these disorders. If we can identify and relieve the anger issues, the individual experiences a feeling of accomplishment, success, self-understanding and encouragement that other problems can be solved as well.

Substance abusers may not even be aware that they are angry. That is part of the problem. Their addictive behavior has "succeeded" in solving their anger problems by numbing them out.

This is not success, but suppression. The anger problem has not gone away but remains down below the level of conscious awareness. It continues to go undiagnosed and untreated. It cannot get better and it will only get worse.

Anger is an energy. It is not static, but dynamic. When we feel inadequate to cope with our anger problems, we try to stuff this anger down inside ourselves and to keep it there. It is down there, all right, but it isn't standing still. It is turning into physical and emotional symptoms that are worse than the original anger problem ever was. These anger-born symptoms often give rise to depression and anxiety, which means that the substance abusers now have two problems and they must be "dual diagnosed" to receive proper treatment.

It is safe to assume that these addicts are angry at the people who have hurt them. They may deny that they are angry -- they are "just hurt." We can expose their anger by asking a focusing question: *"How do you feel towards the people who hurt you?"* Angry.

In dredging this anger up into the sunlight, we are accomplishing several positive purposes. We are relieving the pressure that it takes to keep the anger down there, freeing this energy for more productive purposes. We are calling their emotion by its rightful name and giving them permission to have this human emotion that they were told as children they weren't supposed to have. In addition, we are validating them as worthwhile human beings in spite of it. No one ever did that for them before.

After we have established the fact that they are angry, and that their anger is legitimate and permissible, we need to ask another focusing question: *"Who else are you angry at?"* They are often angry at themselves, but this anger is inaccessible. It is buried under the more obvious anger at the other people in their lives. It is this self-anger that creates an insoluble problem. "How can I relieve my anger at myself for all the stupid things I have done in my life?" Since this question is unanswerable, these individuals feel inadequate to cope and they feel out of control. These feelings are painful, and the task of relieving this pain becomes still another problem that these people cannot solve.

Their substance abuse can be understood, to some extent, as their way of solving an insoluble problem and numbing out the pain of their existence, which they do not know how to relieve in any other way. They hold themselves in contempt, and their self-destructive but negatively exciting behavior is their way of bringing about the fate that "worthless" people deserve. Their self-destruction, then, is the ultimate solution to the ultimate problem.

By respecting these people in spite of their unpleasant anger problems and setting an example of competence and self-respect for them to follow, we can begin to replace their underlying self-contempt with self-respect. They will begin to see that they were not "stupid," "guilty" or "worthless." They were merely imperfect human beings growing up under difficult circumstances. They need not be angry at themselves. There is no self-anger to suppress. If we can relieve the pain of their existence in the right way, they will be free to stop trying to relieve it in the wrong way.

#74. SUICIDE

We do not usually think of suicide as an anger mismanagement technique, but, in a way, that is what it is. We understand suicidal impulses as a component of depression. Depressed people are often angry at themselves for all sorts of "reasons," none of which are rational. These "reasons" often have to do with a problem that they feel unable to solve, a lost love, a lost job or the death of a loved one. These losses are not the problem. The problem may be that the suicidal individuals are angry at themselves for their failure or inability to solve the problem. They do not respect inadequate, incompetent failures who are out of control, who fail to prevent bad things from happening. Such people are worthless. They are worthy to die.

When this self-anger occurs in a context of self-contempt, these people have no resources with which to counteract their impulses to self-destruction. They cannot bear the pain of their existence, which is another problem that they cannot solve. They feel powerless, but there is one power that they have left, the ultimate power -- the power of life and death. Self-murder is their way of overcompensating for their feelings of powerlessness. That is one purpose of their self-destructive behavior. At the same time, they can get revenge on the people who have hurt them by depriving them of their company forever. A third purpose that is served by their suicide is the withdrawal from the tasks of everyday life with which they feel inadequate to cope. These are all negative purposes, and suicide comes under the heading of mischief -- that which does not need to be done. These negative purposes are consistent with their self-contempt.

We can learn how to give suicidal persons emotional first aid when they need it. We do not debate with them over the relative merits of life versus death. Their purposes are not rational, and they cannot be reasoned out of them.

Instead of reacting to them on their territory, we can bring them over to ours. We can control the interchange. We can choose to ask a focusing question: *"What happened to make you angry?"* This question distracts them away from insoluble problems of life and death and gives them soluble problems that they can talk about sensibly. Their depression changes back into anger, which can then be managed and disposed of. Moreover, when they hear themselves being spoken to with respect for their legitimate griefs, their self-contempt loses its grip on them. Its place is often taken by self-respect. When both of these aspects of suicidal feelings are relieved, the pain of their existence goes away. They are free. They have come out of their crisis stronger than when they went in.

#75. SUPPRESSION

Most of us think that managing anger means suppressing it. We have been taught by nonexperts in the field that anger must be controlled. This too turns out to be suppression. We are taught by our anger-illiterate elders to fear our anger. We are a nation of angerphobics. We live in fear that an outward expression of unpleasant emotions will have scary consequences. We are afraid of:

1. Displeasing people.

2. Being abandoned.

3. Losing control.

4. Being victimized.

5. Being annihilated.

We are not consciously aware of these fears, for we have suppressed those, too. Yet, our fears determine our behavior just the same. When someone wakes us at three a.m and asks, "Did I wake you?" we do not even think of expressing our anger. We lie and say, "No, I wasn't sleeping, just dozing a little." We are so well trained that we can not even feel the anger that this intrusion must have caused us. That is true suppression.

A Pain We Cannot Feel

Anger and fear are painful, and we feel inadequate to cope with these emotions. They create problems for us that we do not know how to solve. We try to solve painful problems by suppressing them down below the level of conscious awareness. We coat them over like an oyster with a pearl. But the problems are still down there, for the pain has not gone away we just can't feel it anymore. It sounds like an oxymoron to say that we have a pain that we cannot feel, but it is the truth. We can tell that the pain is still down there by the shadow that it casts over our lives. It keeps us from being as happy and successful as we have the right to be. It interferes with our relationships and makes us abandon people before they can abandon us, which makes no sense at all. Our pain predisposes us to be on constant guard against further pain, and it seduces us into living in the future so that we can prevent disasters from happening in advance. These are just a few of the absurdities of everyday life, and they all derive from the pain of our existence -- a pain that we cannot even feel. Our silent attitudes towards anger have created emotional problems that we are inadequately prepared to solve.

When we replace our painful feelings of self-doubt and inadequacy to cope with feelings of self-respect, these fears are overcome. We have the courage to take the risks that life requires us to take. That includes the risk of expressing our legitimate anger appropriately. It takes courage to say, *"It makes me angry when you do that."* When we make it happen, we feel in control, independent, mature and competent, all of which are facets of self-respect.

When we write an anger letter to someone who has caused us a grievance, we tap into the pool of residual anger that goes back to our earliest years. It starts to pour out on the page in a tangible, concrete form. Our anger is manageable at last and we have the adult resources now to manage it. As we do this anger homework in the real world -- not the world of fears of overcompensations -- we undo the effects of a lifetime of suppression. We have earned the right to feel secure within ourselves, confident that we can succeed again and liberated from the frightened, inadequate child we used to be. We learn to trust our ability to cope with strong emotions with which we could not cope in childhood.

"No matter how cynical I get, I can't keep up."

Lily Tomlin

#76. SWEARING

Swearing is an immature anger management technique that we acquired in second grade and carried intact into adulthood. People are rarely impressed by the swearer's sophistication, intelligence and command of the English language.

Excessive swearing is a symptom of self-contempt. When people use scatological language, they are holding their mother tongue in the same contempt that they hold themselves. They are revealing their personal and linguistic bankruptcy.

The antidote to this lingual abuse is self-respect. Self-respecting people do not use language that demeans their hearers as well as themselves. They do not sink to using lowest common denominator vocabulary, nor do they strive for overcompensatory verbal pyrotechnics. They communicate in the middle ground between these extremes, even when they are experiencing strong emotion. They respect their hearers as well as themselves and they choose their words accordingly.

Do's and Don'ts

When your children begin using words that they learned in school or from their Uncle Barney, you can choose not to overreact. This phenomenon is not a reflection on your parenting skills or your worth as a person. When you overreact, you are rewarding the behavior and guaranteeing that it will happen again very soon.

Instead of focusing on the child's mischief, you can focus on your anger. When you say, *"That word makes me angry,"* you are not paying off this mischief, but using a logical consequence of the child's misbehavior. Your child does not want you to be angry. The child knows now what will happen the next time. It is no fun at all. If the child tests you again later, you must pass the test. If you overblow, it means that the child has succeeded in getting to you and you will lose leverage. You may up the ante by using a stronger logical consequence, but erupting like a volcano is just paying off the mischief.

This is not to say that we expect parents to stop erupting immediately and forever. That would be perfection. Imperfect parents erupt from time to time. Our hope is that as your self-respect increases, your eruptions will come farther apart and end sooner each time. That is a sign that you are healing. You are a worthwhile human being in the meantime.

#77. TAKE TIME OUT OF TIME

We all suffer from time poverty. There is always too much to do and not enough time to do it. We don't even have time to get angry, so we just stuff it down until we can get home and displace it on the dog or whoever we see first.

We learned as children to put other people first and ourselves second. We have no time for our own legitimate concerns. We run ourselves ragged until we burst a blood vessel. Then we stop running around permanently. We do all this running and chasing because we think we have to. If we sit still, it is a "waste" of productive time and someone will catch up to us and pass us by or someone will say that we are lazy. All our goodness will be for nothing. These are just a few of the mistaken attitudes that propel us into perpetual motion. We are all playing an endless game of "beat the clock." The antidote is to take time out of time. That is very hard for us to do, which is why hardly anyone does it.

Vignette: Be My Guest

Nancy was having a thirtieth birthday party for her husband, Matt. Sister-in-law Greta was there a half hour early as usual, wanting to know where the spoons were and who is going to bring in the cake. Before counseling, Nancy would have said, "Get out of my kitchen. Go out there and enjoy yourself." Instead, Nancy chose to take time out of time. She was not interested in a power struggle with Greta over who was going to be boss in whose kitchen. She agreed with Greta, *"Here, take this ladle and stir the soup."* She took off her apron and went outside to play ball with her two boys and their father who did not ever remember seeing her out of the kitchen before. She had a relaxing half hour before the party instead of playing her usual agonizing role as the "uptight perfectionist." Greta was feeling no pain either. She was in control of the pots and pans. It was a win-win situation and a good time was had by all.

#78. TALK IT OUT

Before there were psychotherapists, there were poets and philosophers trying to teach us the truth about the human condition. One such truth was, "Confession is good for the soul." Confessing our private thoughts and fears is hard to do. If it were easy, we would not need constant reminders to do it.

There are several impediments to talking our anger out:

1. Emotionality is seen as weakness or a loss of control.

2. Anger is unpleasant, and we fear disapproval, rejection and abandonment.

3. We have no parental example of appropriate anger expression to follow.

4. We have not acquired the appropriate verbal terms for the negative feeling in our hearts. We call it "hate," "irritated" or "bothered."

5. Our priorities are backwards. Instead of talking about our legitimate anger, we wallow in the pain it is causing us. We use our pain to get attention from others or to revenge ourselves upon them. We are making verbal mischief instead of talking sense about our human emotions.

6. Write your "reason" here. Ask yourself the focusing questions: *"What is the worst thing that would happen if I talked out my anger? What am I afraid would happen if I did?"* _____
_____.

"Brain architects" tell us that males have fewer links between their left and right hemispheres than females. This is their explanation of the difficulty that "left brain dominant" men have in articulating feelings that arise in the right hemisphere. Women are said to have more neural connections between left and right brain hemispheres so that thoughts and feelings can pass back and forth more easily.

Regardless of neural connections, our experience is that self-respecting people feel freer to talk things out more easily than people who hold themselves in contempt and who feel that they must overcompensate by playing the role of the "tough guy" or the stoic.

Unself-respecting people do not respect their feelings and emotions any more than they respect the rest of their personhood. They have the conviction that their feelings are not worth expressing and that their concerns are unimportant to the significant others in their lives. They cannot risk being invalidated. It would hurt too much, so they keep it in. They do not see why they shouldn't. It is the misery that they prefer to the even worse misery of taking the risk and being humiliated again as they were in childhood.

I was angry with my friend;
I told my wrath,
my wrath did end.
I was angry with my foe;
I told it not,
my wrath did grow.

- William Blake

Do's and Don't's

Encourage people to express their anger in an atmosphere of mutual respect. It helps if you can put the word "anger" in their ear. *"That must have made you angry. I'd be angry if it happened to me."* When they express their anger, do not take it personally. They are only saying that you are imperfect. You can say, *"Good, I'm glad you can tell me that you're angry."* You can now use your focusing question to find out the rest of the story.

The antidote to fear is courage. Self-respecting people are willing to take the risk.

Talking it out does not mean using your negative emotion to get pity and advice from your well-intentioned resources. You have no intention of taking their advice, so save everyone the time and trouble. Instead of being dependent on the judgment of people who were not even there when it happened, practice trusting your own judgment. It isn't perfect, but it is good enough. You will never be independent until you do.

Find out why you cannot talk it out. Ask yourself, *"Where does this come from?"* Very often, a recollection will pop into your conscious mind and you will answer the question.

Another way to find out is to ask yourself, *"How would my life be different if I overcame my fear of talking it out?"* Maybe you would be guilty of disobeying your parents? Maybe you would be happy.

#79. TELL THE TRUTH

Do you see yourself as an honest person who tells the truth? Of course you do. It is so easy to tell the truth when nothing is at stake. You can tell your seven-year-old child that his room is a disgusting mess, but you could not tell your Aunt Celeste that her moustache is growing in again. It would be too unpleasant and it could get you beaten up or, worse, humiliated in the eyes of your family forever. No, there is too much at stake.

Second, we cannot tell the truth if that truth is inconsistent with the role we have been playing all our lives. If we are the "victim" of our family we cannot tell any truth that would bring about the scary, painful victimization that we are trying so hard to prevent. If we are the disgruntled rebel of the bunch, we cannot say, "Thanks, I love this sweater," because it might give the "oppressors" an iota of satisfaction if we did.

This is particularly true of our anger. We are so well trained by now to deny the truth of our anger that, when the opportunity for truthfulness arises, we cannot do it and it passes, often forever. Often, we are not given another chance.

When we are angry, it would be appropriate and therapeutic for us to say, *"It makes me angry when you do that."* That is the truth, but we cannot say it. Our relationships would be more solid and mature if we did, but no one believes that and hardly anyone does it. Instead, we say things like, "You're the dumbest person I've ever seen in my life." That is not the truth, but we are stuck with it.

It takes courage to tell the truth -- that is why we cannot do it when the chips are down. As children, we lacked the courage to overcome our fears. We are adults now, and if we wish to outgrow this baggage from our childhood, we need to make appropriate choices. Courage is the willingness to take a risk. If you can take that risk and tell the truth when you are angry, the truth shall make you free. Instead of saying, "I hate you," which is not true, you can say to a loved one, a friend, a co-worker, *"It makes me angry when you do that,"* or *"I am angry at you."* That is the truth. You are not "upset" or "bothered." These are euphemisms that water down the truth of our emotion. As adults, now, we can use our adult judgment to determine when it is appropriate to "Tell the Truth" or "Give It a Pass." We are not perfect and are not required to tell the truth perfectly every time. We can choose when and to whom we express our anger. This power of choice is a technique called, "Discretion." Self-respecting people use their discretion in a crisis. They do not abuse the privilege. They know what the reality of the situation requires them to do and they do it.

#80. TEMPER TANTRUMS

This is the first entry that most parents will turn to. It is the most common anger management problem that parents have, and most of them feel woefully inadequate to cope with these very unpleasant anger attacks.

On one level, it is very frustrating to be two or three years old and not be able to solve most of your problems. A majority of these problems come under the heading of, "I want my way but I can't figure out how to get it."

The child's anger is painful in itself. It has many components:

1. He confuses his parents' refusal to give him his way as a loss of love.

2. He feels that it is his fault that he is unlovable.

3. He feels that he is worthless.

4. It is his fault that he cannot solve all these problems.

5. He has taken their refusal personally as a wipeout of his fragile personhood.

This spiral of pain is too much for the child to handle. The temper tantrum is the manifestation of his pain and his powerlessness to do anything constructive about it.

The last thing he needs is to have his all important parent compound his grief by treating him like the enemy. Some children pick up this role and run with it.

Parents have feelings, too, feelings of anger, powerlessness, shame and guilt. They too, feel inadequate to cope with the child's inadequacy. Parents do not appreciate being put in a situation which threatens to expose their inadequacy for all the neighbors to see. Under these circumstances, the parents are liable to react to the problem by throwing a countertantrum.

The child, then, has one agenda, the parents have an entirely different one. Parents cannot cope with the child's pain if they are the out-of-control prisoners of their own.

On another level, a temper tantrum can be understood as mischief. It doesn't need to be done. Why do they do it? One purpose of this mischief is to get attention, and it works. The attention is all negative, but it proves to the child that he still exists. A more significant purpose is power and control. The child feels powerless to do anything constructive about his situation, but he sure has the power to provoke his parents to madness. When he succeeds, it relieves the pain of his powerlessness. He pays a high price, but he seems willing to pay it.

Antidote

To save our own sanity, we must first identify the child's negative behavior as mischief and disengage ourselves emotionally from it. It helps if we can identify our personal vulnerabilities to be being sucked into the propellers:

1. "I am taking this tantrum personally, as if it were a reflection on my parenting skills, my competence as a parent and my worth as a human being. *I can choose to remind myself that I*

am still a worthwhile human being in spite of this regrettable happenstance."

2. "I am feeling out of control because I have mistakenly defined control in terms of shutting this kid up instantly and perfectly. *I can remind myself that I have the power of choice. I can choose to be in control of myself. I certainly cannot control him if I am not in control of myself.*"

3. "I want my way and my child is not giving it to me and I cannot make him. I'm as immature as he is. One of us has to grow up and it isn't going to be him. *I can remind myself that I am a worthwhile human being whether my child obeys my commands instantly or not.*"

4. "I am feeling totally responsible for my child and I am doing a lousy job. I feel guilty of the crime of irresponsibility. I have allowed this catastrophe to happen. It is all my fault." *I need to remind myself tha it is not my fault, it is no one's fault. My imperfect child is having a fit, just like everyone else's imperfect child. He is worthwhile in spite of it and so am I.*"

5. "I am vulnerable to worrying about how this looks to the neighbors. I feel like I am being disgraced forever in their eyes." *I need to remind myself that my child is more important to me than these people are. I can choose to live on my terms, not theirs. I can free myself to do what the situation requires me to do.*"

After sorting out this welter of feelings and attitudes, we are in a much better position to solve the problems than we would have been in the old days.

"What does your love entitle you to do to me?"

Rudolph Dreikurs

Do's and Don'ts

Do not get into a power struggle with your child over who can make whom stop doing what. Do not take his behavior as a reflection on you. Do not worry about the neighbors' opinion of you. They have their own problems.

Do not have a countertantrum.

Do not let him play one parent against the other.

Instead, you can remind yourself that you are not out of control. You have the power of choice:.

You can choose to exert firm but gentle restraint upon your child. You can put your arms around him to show him that you are in control, that you are on his side and that you are not going to make his pain worse by abandoning him.

You can choose to ride out the anger storm without overreacting to the provocation.

You can reveal the power component of the tantrum by asking, *"Could it be that you will stop kicking when you are good and ready? Well, that's all right. I can wait."* It will end a lot sooner this way than if you try to shorten the attack the old way by saying, "Stop that this instant. This just gives him more power to defeat you.

In the meantime, you are not out of control, you are not living on his terms but on your own. When he senses that you are in control and refusing to play off his mischief, he will calm down sooner.

You can send him to his room, not as punishment, but as "quiet time" so that he can cool down his sensory overload. It breaks the cycle of frustration. You can say, *"We will talk about it when you feel better."*

Later on, you can ask the focusing question, *"What angered you the most when I wouldn't buy you the ten-pound chocolate bar?"*

"You never buy me anything."

"It seems that way sometimes, doesn't it."

"You don't love me."

"I'm sorry you feel that way."

"I don't love you."

"I don't blame you for being angry."

"You hate me.

"What you do makes me angry sometimes."

You are not required to defend, explain, account or justify. You are validating the child's worth in spite of his faults and imperfections, one of which is that he hasn't yet learned how to manage his anger. You can use this painful episode as an opportunity to teach him what he needs to know about anger.

"The next time you get so angry at me, I want you to say, "It makes me angry when you don't do this for me."

"Is it all right for me to be angry at you?"

"Yes, it isn't all right to get upset in the Dominick's where people are trying to do their shopping. You have a choice now. Can you remember to say that next time?"

"If I forget, will you remind me?"

"I'd be happy to."

This is not controlling or suppressing. This is revealing to him that he has a choice. This is empowering the child to solve his anger problem. This is the antidote to his powerlessness.

#81. THIRD CHOICE TECHNIQUE

When we feel frustrated, we feel powerless and out of control plus angry. We feel trapped, like there is no way out, with no solution to the problem in sight. We have no choice or, what is worse, we have two choices and we hate them both. If our boss, Harry, makes us angry, we can choose to explode in his face and get fired or we can stuff our anger inside our chest as we usually do.

We are not really powerless and out of control. We just feel that way most of the time. We have a power called the "Third Choice" technique. Instead of tearing our brains in half over these two unacceptable options, we can use our adult creativity to give ourselves a third option. *"I know, I'll write Harry an anger letter and then tear it up. I can even choose to write a second letter that I can put on his desk."*

When we have two unacceptable choices, we have an insoluble problem. We turn the problem around and around in our mind trying to solve it. We call this mental merry-go-round obsessing and we will never solve the problem that way. We need some new input. We need a third choice.

Vignette: Solving the Insoluble Problem:

Mary Lou and Zack were having a quarrel. Zack had forgotten his keys again and had to wait an hour for her to come home. He had even forgotten that the spare key was hidden in the mailbox. When Mary Lou drove up and saw him sitting on the doorstep like a forlorn puppy, she blew up. "That's the third time you've locked yourself out of the house. You are so irresponsible. You were the baby of your family and you're still the baby. You just can't cope. You can't solve problems."

As usual, Zack began defending himself at her expense. He pointed out her recent lapses and faux pas at the top of his voice. This was his approach to problem-solving -- drown it out so that you can't hear it. Mary Lou opened the door and they went in, but their evening together got off on the wrong foot and it stayed that way.

In counseling, Mary Lou admitted that she was at an impasse. She knew that criticizing Zack only made it worse, but she could not keep her anger in, for it would make her sick. She would have a splitting headache in the morning.

Mary Lou had for some time been saying, "I am angry at you, Zack," and he was beginning to take her more seriously and to cooperate with her. She was pleased with her progress and did not want to derail it. She did not want to wear out her "I" Message technique.

Oppositionality

Luckily, there was another choice open to her. Mary Lou saw a pattern of irresponsibility in Zack, but she also saw a pattern of defensiveness and opposition to whatever she said. When May Lou confronted Zack about his "againstness," he simply said, "That's just the way I am," which is his way of saying that he has no intention of looking into his own motivations or changing himself to accommodate her. It is another example of his oppositionalty.

The truth is that this is not the way he is at all. This is just a role that he has been playing since he was two. He never outgrew his "terrible twos" oppositionality because it kept working. It kept his parents hopping and now it is doing the same thing to his wife. He thinks that he is in control and that he is winning these battles, but it is only mischief.

We can choose to stop focusing on Zack's regrettable irresponsibility and to stop trying to make him agree with us. We cannot force him to see things our way, for he is afraid that he would lose his shaky identity if he did.

Instead, we decided to focus on Zack's oppositionality for the sake of being oppositional. Mary Lou learned how hard it was for Zack to let go of his own position, even if it was absurd. His position in the argument was not the issue. His worth as a person was at stake and that was the issue.

That night, they were having a conversation between two grown-up human beings when Mary Lou mentioned the key incident. *"You must have been very angry at being locked out."* She was trying to validate his anger and encourage him to express it in more productive ways. Zack's fragile veneer of maturity cracked and he went into his role as the oppositional child, "You're nuts, I wasn't angry. It didn't bother me at all." Here is where the third choice comes in. Mary Lou could have chosen to rebut his absurdly false statement or she could have chosen to bite her tongue and suppress her feelings. She chose a third course, to change the subject, *"It's hard for you to agree with me, isn't it, Zack?"*

"No, it isn't."

"There, Zack. You just did it again. You can't even agree with me that it's hard to agree." She had caught him in the act, which made it hard for Zack to deny that he had just done what he did. She was not criticizing or forcing, she was just talking to him in a new key, as one equal member of the human race to another.

"It's always been hard for me to agree with people and I never knew why," said Zack.

"What's the hardest thing about agreeing, Zack?"

"I feel like I won't be myself if I take someone else's side. I'll be giving up something of myself."

"Do you define yourself in terms of your position on these matters? I don't. I am a worthwhile human being in spite of my faults and imperfections, whether people agree with me or not. I am even worthwhile if I agree with them. Maybe they know something that I don't know. I trust them and I trust myself. I don't have nearly as many battles as you do."

"Isn't that giving in?"

"No. It is cooperating with my fellow human beings in getting the job done, whatever it is. I do not confuse cooperation with submission. I do not rebel, I am a worthwhile human being either way. Isn't that a better basis for getting along with people, as an equal?"

"It's hard to say it, but maybe you're right."

"That's good, Zack. I'm glad you feel that way. That makes me happy. Was it as hard as you thought it would be?"

"No. It wasn't. Maybe I can do it again sometime."

"Who made that happen just now?"

"I did."

"So you didn't lose yourself, did you? In fact, you found yourself. That is a feeling of identity, maturity and independence. You are liberating yourself from your childhood roles. You have the power of choice now. You can choose to agree or disagree. Before, you only had one choice."

"You're right. I feel better now."

"What did it cost you to agree with me?"

"Nothing. Just the excitement that I used to get from stirring up things. I don't need that any more."

"That's right. It doesn't cost you anything that you really need. Can you do it again?"

"Sure I can."

"That is called confidence. You cannot have confidence if you are always playing a role opposite some one else's role. Isn't this a pleasanter way to live your life?"

"Yes, it is."

"You see? You just agreed with me again. You're getting good at this. You could learn to love it."

First Choice	Second Choice	Third Choice
The Lesser Misery	The Greater Misery	No Misery At All
Pleasing everyone so they will like me.	Displeasing everyone and being rejected.	*Being an independent person on my own terms and pleasing myself as a worthwhile human being.*
Preventing disaster by controlling.	Letting go of control, which is scary.	*Taking life as it comes and doing the best I can with it.*

First Choice	Second Choice	Third Choice
The Lesser Misery	The Greater Misery	No Misery At All
Submitting on my knees.	Rebelling and being shot down.	*Cooperating as an equal member of the human race.*
Not wanting to be like my mother.	Fearing that I will go to the opposite extreme, which would be worse.	*Living in the middle ground between the two extremes like a self-respecting human being.*
To keep trying harder and harder.	To stop trying and give up in discouragement.	*To stop trying so hard and just do what reality requires -- no more and no less.*
To keep proving that I am always right and never wrong.	To admit I am wrong and give up the fight.	*To accept myself as an imperfect human being as I am right now.*
To live in fear of abandonment.	To get it over with and abandon others before they can abandon me.	*To respect myself as a worthwhile human being with an identity of my own. As long as I have myself, I can never be abandoned. I can stop worrying about it.*
To keep trying to make them understand me.	To find someone new who might understand me better.	*To begin learning how to understand myself.*

Do's and Don'ts

Do not fight against these conflicting choices. They are based on attitudes from childhood. You cannot fight them or reason them away. You can simply break their grip on you by replacing them with healthier choices based on attitudes that derive from mature, independent self-respect.

#82. TURN THE OTHER CHEEK

"If an evildoer smite thee on the cheek, turn the other to him also, for a soft answer turneth away wrath." (Luke 6:29) (see #20, Do the Unexpected; #18, Disengage from the Mischief; #16, Discretion; #81, Third Choice Technique).

#83. UNDERSTANDINGNESS

We are all in favor of improved "understanding," and we all imagine that we understand ourselves. But what is it called when someone who does not understand the other person's attitudes and predispositions tries to make that person understand something they do not want to understand? This absurd good intention can be called "understandingness."

Very often, when Herman and Florence are fighting, their anger attack consists of two parties trying to pound sense into the other's skull at the expense of the other person's self-respect. Herman is implying that, until Florence understands "the truth" as he has defined it, she is a dummy. He cannot improve his partner's receptivity to his ideas by placing her in a one down position. She will try to relieve the pain of her inferiority by doing the same thing to him. An amicable exchange of views is impossible under these conditions.

A good technique, then, would be to catch ourselves trying desperately to make the other person understand us by yelling in their ear. We can choose to stop in our tracks. We are now free to do something else, something that might work better. We can disengage from their mischief and our own. Trying to make someone understand against their will is mischief -- it does not need to be done. Instead of waiting for people to "understand," we can tell the truth right now, *"It makes me angry when you do that."* This is a simple, declarative sentence. They can understand it. We can choose not to elaborate, account or explain ourselves to them. We can set an example of constructive, appropriate behavior for them to see and follow. They may not understand in their head why they are following our new example; maybe they will just understand in their hearts. In any case, your life will go on whether they understand or not -- you are worthwhile either way.

#84. VALIDATE, VALIDATE, VALIDATE

One of the purposes of this book is to show you how you can use an adverse, unpleasant situation like an anger attack to earn for yourself the feeling that you are a worthwhile, competent human being. If you work it right, an anger problem can be an opportunity to heal and grow, not just on the outside or for the sake of the relationship, but inside your own selfhood, which is where you live.

First, you validate your partner's anger. *"I am sorry you are so angry."* Second, by saying that, you validate them as worthwhile, acceptable human beings in spite of their faults and imperfections, one of which is that they get angry from time to time. The third "validation" is for you. You have solved the problem constructively. You have put your money where your mouth is and you have had the courage to reach out and intervene effectively. You have earned the right and the joy of feeling like a self-respecting human being. You have used an anger situation constructively. You have treated your partner with respect under difficult circumstances and you have solved an interpersonal relationship problem that you could not solve before. This successful accomplishment gives you confidence that you can do it again. You were not playing a role, you had an independent, mature identity of your own.

"Like all mischief, good intentions are self-indulgent, counter-productive and self destructive."

Rudolph Dreikurs

This is what we call, "Emotional First Aid." Not only have you relieved your partner's pain, but you have relieved your own. You have had a real intention and did what reality required. You have overcome your self-doubt and replaced it with self-respect. You have stopped the bleeding.

#85. THE VICTIM

As children, we were vulnerable to perceiving the bad things that happened to us as if they were personal victimizations. We took our deprivations and grievances personally, as a loss of self-worth.

Now, as adults, we have the same predisposition to play the victim role when there is no victimization. For instance, when we do not get a promotion, we feel unfairly deprived, victimized and out of control. This unfairness makes us angry, but our definition of unfair is not objective, it is subjective. "Fairness means getting my way. Life is unfair to me when I don't get my way. How can they do this to me?" The managers feel that they have promoted the better employee on the basis of objective considerations. But we are not interested in objectivity or real fairness. We have our own private considerations, grievances and anger. We are a victim looking for a place to happen, and it just happened. This negative situation has confirmed us in our unhappy role. This is not living, this is merely existing.

The "tip-off" to "The Victim Syndrome" lies in the words, "to me." That is the victim talking. Our antidote to playing this childish role from kindergarten such as "The teacher held up everyone's picture but mine. Why me?" is our self-respect. We can replace our unhappy role as the victim with an identity as a worthwhile human being whether we get our way or not. We can say to ourselves, *"Could it be that I am perceiving victimization where no victimization is intended? Even if it is intended, I am still not a victim, I am a worthwhile human being in spite of it, no more and no less than anyone else."*

THE VICTIM

Coping With The Victim

When someone is angry at you for causing them a grievance, being late, divorcing them or firing them from their job because the plant is closing, you can assume that there is an element of victimhood in their rage, If there is not, there is no harm done, but there usually is. This perception of personal victimization makes their pain worse than it needs to be.

You can relieve their painful overreaction to the reality situation by identifying the victim component to them. They are not aware that they are playing this role as such, for they have been doing it for years. It comes natural to them now. You can say, *"I am sorry that you are feeling victimized by all this,"* and that is true. You regret that it is happening. This does not mean that you caused the victimization.

Or, you can say, *"Could it be that you are perceiving this as a victimization? Well, it really isn't. It's regrettable. I wish that it weren't happening, but you are not a victim, you are a worthwhile human being in spite of it. On that basis, you can get on with your life and do even better than you have done before."* That is emotional first aid. You haven't cured them of their predisposition to feel victimized, but you have treated them with respect in spite of their imperfections.

Vignette: Victim Of Waste

Penny knew that her husband Dick had been victimized as a child. She knew that he was still predisposed to perceive things as victimization when they were not. She was twenty minutes late for a rare lunch date with him downtown. He was furious when she got there. "Wasting time" makes him angry, feeling out of control makes him angry and perceiving himself as the victim of her tardiness makes him the angriest of all. She didn't defend herself because she knew that she was not the issue and time

wasn't the issue, his anger was the issue. She had learned to say, *"I'm sorry that you are feeling victimized by my lateness, but that was not my intention. I don't blame you for being angry."* She did not say it in a patronizing, pseudo-clinical way, as if she were talking to a problem child. She had the right words and the right music. She had disengaged from Dick's mischief, but not from him. She spoke to him as one imperfect human being to another.

Dick was able to let go of his anger and fear of being hurt by someone he loved, as he had been hurt so many times when he was growing up. His anger subsided and he felt understood and validated. With Penny's help, his role as his wife's victim was being replaced with an identity of his own as a worthwhile human being. They went on with their lunch.

Vignette: Victim Of A Victim

Gina met Woodie at a singles dance. He was charming. They seemed to hit it off from the very start. He was from out of town and had no family here, just a few friends. For the first few months, everything was fine. Then they started to argue, as couples do. After a few more months, he began beating her. Gina didn't think too much of it because she had seen her father hit her mother plenty of times. "That's what involved people do. They hit each other."

The beatings got worse. She lost her feelings for him and wanted to break up. He stalked her on her way home from work. She became afraid of him. She was not his lover anymore, she was his victim.

In counseling, Gina learned to see Woodie as someone who perceived himself as "Life's Victim." In his eyes, everyone was against him and for no good reason. He could never see how he contributed to the negative things that happened to him. It was never his fault.

That weekend he called her on the phone for a date, as charming as he was the night they met. Gina had learned to identify this tactic as "The Old Charmeroo" and she knew how dangerously deceptive it was.

She arranged to see him so that she could tell him in person that it was over. That was her first mistake. She should have told him right then on the phone. He insisted on changing their rendezvous from a neighborhood cafe to a fancier restaurant out in the country. She went along with it in order to avoid "displeasing" him. That was her second mistake. She should have stayed with her original agenda instead of surrendering control to him. Her "pleasingness" set her up to be victimized by this self-styled "victim." He was in control and he was going to use his control destructively. This is the only way he knows how to use it. It is consistent with his self-contempt.

Woodie got her out in the country, away from everyone. He was angry at her for not giving him his way, for depriving him of her company and for inconveniencing him. In his eyes, these "offenses" constituted victimization and he felt entitled to punish her for her "crimes" against him.

He hit her harder than he ever had before. She was truly frightened and she knew that she was in big trouble. Fortunately for her, she had learned to disengage from mischief and to do the unexpected. Instead of yelling and screaming, which he would see as another rejection, another "victimization," she asked herself, *"What is the last thing he expects me to do?"* He expected her to accuse him of hurting her, to order him to stop or to threaten him with the law, which she knew was a joke. She did not do any of these useless things. She talked about herself, not in a self-pitying way, which could only invite more abuse and scorn, but in a new way, as a person in her own right. She was making it happen, *"I'm all right, It's OK, I'm fine."* She was reassuring him that she was not going to get revenge on him and that he wasn't going to succeed in provoking her into doing anything that would give him an excuse for more madness.

He pushed her out of the car and drove off. She walked to a gas station and called a cab. She never saw him again. She knows that he is still out there, doing it again to his next victim, but there is nothing she can do to prevent it. Some problems cannot be solved. That is regrettable. But she is alive and out of harms way. She is not a victim or a pleaser anymore. These roles have been replaced with an well-earned identity as a worthwhile human being in her own right. She is not compatible with victimizers anymore. She is compatible with self-respecting human beings.

#86. VIOLENCE

What has been the scourge of the twentieth century? Not cancer, AIDS, drug abuse or heart disease, but violence. More people have died violently in this century than in any other. There is no basis for assuming that the next century will be any less violent because we are not taking any steps to make it so.

Every year, there are a million and a quarter reported acts of violence. Some are fatal, some merely result in permanent injury or disfigurement. Others end in the orphaning of children and the widowing of spouses. There are public and private agencies attempting to deal with the plague of violence in our country, but their focus seems to be on the overt act, such as firing handguns or battering a spouse or a child. If they can prevent these acts, they feel that they will have prevented violence. The underlying issues that predisposed the individual to solving problems violently have not been identified or addressed.

Another mistake that we make is to treat violence or aggression as if they were irresistible natural forces -- animal instincts over which mere mortals have no power. Bullies have been using this excuse for years. It exempts them from the consequences of their self-indulgent behavior. We have seen such "irresistible forces" turned off like a light switch by a phone call from a good buddy down at the saloon. We need to stop taking these self-serving alibis at face value if we hope to break the cycle of violence leading to violence.

The cycle is not transmitted by our genetic inheritance from the lower orders, it is modelled for us by the significant others in our young lives. We learn to accept brutality as an efficient problem-solving technique. It requires no cerebral exertion at all. When we grow up, we can hardly wait to pass it on to our children. We feel justified in doing so. "If it was good enough for me, it's good enough for them. That's fair." We cannot argue with this infantile logic. It is not rational logic, but the nonrational logic of attitudes and convictions from childhood.

It should be noted, however, that this learning by example is not absolute. Some children of nonviolent parents become violent on their own. Conversely, many children of violent parents reject this brutal example. Some go to the extreme of crusading actively against violence, while others find the middle ground between the extremes where they can solve interpersonal problems cooperatively as equal members of the human race.

Still other adult children of emotionally or physically violent parents would like to choose the middle ground between excessive violence and grim repression. They do not have the freedom to do so.

These individuals have a pool of forbidden rage that is out of their conscious control; it erupts unpredictably, and it controls their relationships, their jobs and their lives. It provokes them to behave in ways that they despise.

After each firestorm, they feel sincerely guilty and ashamed. They feel weak and worthless. They beg for forgiveness and another chance. They resolve that it will never happen again, only to feel desolate when the next attack overcomes them. Nothing has changed.

Their anger seems to have a life of its own, but it does not. These people must be prepared to endure the pain of resurrecting their subterranean anger. When this anger is brought to the surface and drained properly, not just papered over, the energy that was bound up becomes available for more productive purposes. The wound is allowed to heal cleanly, and the unbidden anger attacks cease to recur. The cycle has been broken.

There is no instinct for beating up first-graders. If there were, everyone would be doing it, not just bullies. Civilized human beings take the time and trouble to learn how to manage their emotions. The problem is that hardly anyone is teaching it these days. We should be teaching young people how to express their anger appropriately in the middle ground between too much and too little. We should teach them how to identify the underlying attitudes that predispose them to taking grievances more personally than they need to be taken.

We all have buttons that can be pushed, such as:

"I want my way and you're not giving it to me."

"Your unfairness makes me angry."

"Your wrongness makes me angry."

"You are going to abandon me."

"You do not appreciate me, I feel good for nothing."

"You are victimizing me."

These attitudes from childhood make us vulnerable to becoming angrier than we need to be. We call this state, "super anger." If these attitudes can be identified and put in a more moderate perspective, we would be less vulnerable to overreacting and our violence statistics would come down. As it is now, we are not well educated in these matters because we are denying that we have an anger problem. We prefer to call our problem "violence," "frustration" or "disgruntled." As a consequence of our denial, we are a nation with a high rate of anger illiteracy.

The issue is not violence or aggression, the issue is mismanaged anger. There is no violence without anger. Violence is an emotional response to a grievance squared or even cubed. Our epidemic of mass murders and serial killings are not "senseless crimes," they are anger crimes. Most of the perpetrators have been through the medico-legal system which keeps turning them loose with their anger undiagnosed and untreated. They have even warned their psychiatrists that they will become violent again, even kill again, but the system spits them out anyway. The present system refuses to hear their cry for help. It does not seem to know what to do about anger except to dope people up or wrap them in cold wet sheets until their anger subsides. Nothing has been learned by anyone.

Many experts see a connection between substance abuse and violence. It may be true that these chemicals stimulate the part of the brain that mediates emotion and that depressants temporarily suspend inhibitions against acting out. It is our conviction that substance abusers were filled with unresolved rage before they became intoxicated and that their anger should have been worked through and relieved beforehand. Mismanaged anger is painful, and these people are trying to relieve their pain by escaping into anesthetics.

We recommend that as many students as possible be given fifteen minutes each week in their Social Studies class for the study of anger. Teachers should be given in-service training on how to teach anger management skills. This will prepare them in advance to cope with anger situations when they arise. After they arise it will be too late. We think that this is a better solution to the violence problem than metal detectors and armed guards in the hallways, which does nothing to prevent the murder of students by students.

Unprepared teachers feel inadequate to cope with student anger, and angry students can sense their vulnerability. Through this training, these feelings of inadequacy can be replaced with feelings of competence to cope with anger situations. When students see teachers coping effectively with their problems, they are more inclined to respect what the teachers have to say, and classroom management problems in general decrease. It is these unresolved anger problems in the classrooms, halls and on the playground that make the educator's task more difficult and painful than it needs to be.

Do's and Don'ts

If you have a violence problem in your home, classroom or place of business, do not let yourself be drawn into a power struggle over who can or cannot hit whom. The overt violence is a symptom of anger. Do not deal with symptoms, for they are just telling us that there is something wrong farther down. Do not protest the "unfairness" of an assault or defend your innocence -- these are not the issues, the issue is that the assaulter is angry. Validate the anger by saying, *"I'm sorry that you are so angry,"* or *"It makes you angry when that happens, doesn't it?"* *"I don't blame you for being angry."*

Focus on the Rage

Ask a focusing question, *"What happened to make you so angry?"* Even if you do not get an answer right away, you have validated the anger and the individual. You have done the unexpected, which disrupts the assaulter's scenario. Ask the next question, *"What angered you the most?"* These questions are relevant whether the violence is directed outward or inward against the self.

Give the individual an alternative outlet for the out-of-control anger. You can even ask, *"What would you like to do instead?"* Let them tell you what their choices are. Often, if they can talk it out, they will not have to do it. The antidote to their frustration is the power of choice. We can give them the gift of choice.

Using your focusing questions, peel the individual's anger artichoke all the way down if you can. After you have focused on their anger at those who caused the precipitating grievance, you can ask, *"Who else are you angry at?"* In almost every case of violence, the assaulters are angry at themselves for some "failure" or "weakness" for which they blame themselves. This is their self-contempt. The formula for violence then is unmanageable self-anger in a context of self-contempt. The antidote consists of replacing the self-contempt with a feeling of self-respect as a worthwhile human being in spite of one's faults and imperfections. At the same time, mismanaged anger is tamed and replaced by appropriate anger expressed appropriately.

Sometimes the violence is due to a brain tumor or other organic cause. The individual who is chronically violent without a precipating factor should be seen by a competent neurologist. Your responsibility is only to make an appropriate referral and to follow up on it.

Do not take the anger personally, as if it were a reflection on your worth as a person. That step makes you vulnerable to being victimized. Self-respecting persons who are in control of themselves and confident in their ability to cope are less likely to be victimized than people who doubt their self-worth.

Do not protect violent people from the consequences of their negative behavior. Do not make excuses for them -- that is enabling. They behave violently because they can; someone is letting them. Use a system of logical consequences, "If this happens, then that will happen," and make it stick. It takes courage because violence is scary. If we give in to our fears, the violence will win and everyone will lose.

#87. WALK AWAY

Walking away from anger sounds easy enough to do, except that there are many wrong ways to walk away and very few right ones. Walking away the wrong way means that someone lost out and that someone suffered a loss of self-respect.

Walking away with a harpoon through your gizzard means that you forgot to disengage from someone's mischief. It's too late to walk away, they have already zinged you. Slinking away like a naughty six-year-old child means that you have taken someone's angry accusation more personally than you needed to take it.

For instance, walking away in self-rightous indignation is one of the wrong ways, as is slinking away like a thief in the night. We are not impressed by these performances, these over-compensations or undercompensations which reveal the individual's obvious lack of preparation to cope with someone's legitimate anger. Self-respecting people know how to validate anger and solve the problem. They do not have to walk away in these counterproductive ways.

The right way to walk away is to disengage from someone's mischief. If the other person's anger is couched in mischief, such as criticizing, complaining, judging, accusing and so on, we can remember that we are under no obligation to stand there and enable them to abuse us. If they are prepared to express their grievances in a mature, businesslike way, we will be glad to hear them out and cooperate with them in resolving our differences. But if they are only interested in building themselves up by tearing us down, we are free to make other arrangements. We can say, *"I'm sorry you're so angry. I have to leave now, but maybe we can talk about it later when you are feeling better."* If they never feel better, then we are off the hook. In any case, it is our right and responsibility to declare our independence from these immature shenanigans. We are not walking out as a reaction to their offensive terms, we are walking out on our own valid terms. They can tell the difference. They will respect us more if we do it the right way.

#88. WHAT DIFFERENCE DOES IT MAKE?

This is a quick and easy focusing question for sorting out anger sense from nonsense. Most of us react to an anger provocation as if it made a difference in our lives, when most of the time it is only kid stuff that doesn't amount to a hill of beans. If it makes a difference, that is one thing. If it does not, it is an entirely different matter and your response will change accordingly.

Vignette: What Will the Neighbors Think?

A suburban couple with two young children were eating Sunday dinner in their favorite restaurant. Scott, the youngest, began to sort out his lima beans from his corn so that he could eat each vegetable separately at his leisure. He has been doing this since his highchair days, which ended more than four years ago. His mother, an otherwise sensible and competent young woman, let out a blast that could be heard in the parking lot. "What are you doing that for? Didn't I tell you to stop playing with your food and just eat your succotash like a normal person?"

Being allergic to child abuse, a diner at a nearby table arose and offered the distraught parent his assistance. *"I know his behavior bothers you, madam, but please tell me this. What difference does it make if he eats his succotash all mixed together or separated into its respective components?"*

"It will take all night. We can't sit here forever."

"Ah! Do you have a pressing engagement later this evening?"

"No. We're not really going to do anything, just go home."

"Then I repeat, what difference does it make?"

"I feel like everyone in the room is watching this kid sort out his beans and corn and I just can't stand it."

"May I say, madam, that no one in this restaurant gives a damn about your child's succotash but you. They are more perturbed by your reaction than by anything your child is doing. I hate to disappoint you, but your child just isn't that important to them."

"I don't want him to grow up playing with his food like that."

"Do you imagine that you can prevent this regrettable outcome by screaming at a six-year-old child?"

"No. I guess it doesn't work."

"What difference will it make if he grows up to be a confirmed food sorter?"

"His wife will think I did a terrible job of training him."

"You are worried twenty years in advance about the opinion of a woman who may not even have been born yet?"

"It does sound pretty silly when you put it that way."

"What difference will it make if she thinks you did a poor job of raising her husband?"

"She won't like me."

"She won't like you if you drive him nuts with your screaming. In any case, it will be her problem from then on, won't it."

"Yes, and I wish her all the luck in the world with his succotash."

"The truth is, that it doesn't make any difference at all how he eats his side dishes. The child cannot control very much in his little world, but he certainly can control his veggies. If you leave him alone, he will come to replace this infantile form of carbohydrate control with more mature, appropriate forms of control in the real world."

"What if he doesn't outgrow it?"

"What difference will it make? What is more important, preventing disaster 20 years from now or having a pleasant dinner with your loved ones in the present? The issue is not table manners. The issues are control, perfectionism, living in the future, fear of failure and feelings of inferiority. You are trying to relieve your painful self-doubts at your child's expense. Your good intentions for him cannot make things better, only worse."

"What can I do?"

"Now that is a good question. You can exercise your power of choice. You can choose to let go of your child's eating habits. You can choose to accept him as a worthwhile human being in the present, in spite of his little faults and imperfections."

"How will that help?"

"It will give you some relief from the pressure and stress that you are putting yourself under. You will set an example of self-acceptance and self-respect for your child to follow."

"Will that make a difference?"

"That will make all the difference in the world."

#89. WHEN IN DOUBT, ASK

When we think someone is angry at us, but we aren't sure, we are often reluctant to find out. We are afraid that asking will only make things worse. So we tiptoe around, hoping it will all go away. This is not a good technique.

Telling people to communicate their concerns to one another is good advice. The question is, why don't they take it? If they took it, we wouldn't have to keep telling them to communicate.

The answer is that communication takes courage and many people do not have the courage to break the sound barrier in their own homes. They take the easy way out. They walk on eggshells forever. They may never find out that it would have been easier to do it the hard way.

Vignette: The Silent Insult

Ron and Grace were expecting company that evening. Ron suggested that Grace straighten out the kitchen, fix lunch and vacuum the living room while he got the recreation room ready.

A half hour later, Grace looked up to see Ron plugging in the vacuum cleaner. "He did it to me again," she thought. He gives me a list of chores to do and then does them himself if I'm not quick enough to suit him." She was sure Ron's behavior was a silent criticism of her housekeeping skill and that he was angry as usual at her slowness.

This time, however, she didn't suffer and stew in silence. Instead of trying to guess at Ron's motivation, she had the courage to ask him what was really going on. Her hurt and anger showed in her voice. Ron did not take her hostile questioning personally. He realized that there was a misunderstanding somewhere. He did not defend himself against her implied accusation that he was silently finding fault with her. He just told the truth about himself, *"I got through early, so I decided to do the vacuuming myself."*

Grace was glad she had asked. She wished that she had been a little less intense, but it could have been a lot worse. They could have had a screaming fight over something that had not happened in the real world, only in her head. Ron was glad, too, that he didn't overreact to her provocation. He chose not to say, "You're so sensitive!" It never helped before and it wouldn't have helped now. Grace's question cleared the air, it relieved her pain and she felt in control of herself again. She thought to herself, "I ought to do that more often."

#90. WHERE DOES THAT COME FROM? HOW TO BREAK THE TRANSFERENCE

Many of your grievances arise out of a transference from some negative person in the past to someone in your present who may not be negative at all. For instance, you may remember your father scolding you terribly for losing a quarter, when money was tight. Now, Herman is complaining about the cost of your gall-bladder medicine. The old money attitudes and fears come to the fore and you behave now as you did then, by crying, defending and generally overreacting to the provocation. He cannot understand where this emotionality comes from and neither can you.

When this happens and neither of you can see any basis in the present for an exaggerated anger attack, it is helpful if one or the other can ask a focusing question such as, *"Where does that come from?"*

Very often this question will evoke a relevant recollection in which the answer to the mystery is embedded.

"Oh, I don't know. Wait, I remember one time when I was seven, my father sent me to the store for a quart of milk. On the way home, I dropped a dime. It rolled into the grass. I got down and looked for it. I was afraid of what my parents would do if I came home without it. They'd think I had stolen it. I didn't realize that it had gotten darker. My father came looking for me. I was still down on my hands and knees. He dragged me home, as I knew he would, scolding me all the way. When I got home, mom took over. The issue wasn't the money. They were trying to teach me responsibility, but they only taught me to hate myself for being so stupid. Now, when you talk about the money I have to spend on myself, all these feelings of guilt and worthlessness come flooding back."

"Now that you know where your feelings are coming from, what can you do about it?"

"I can catch myself going back to being seven-year-old child again. I can choose to remind myself that I am a grown-up now and that I have adult judgment and competencies. I can remember to feel like a worthwhile human being in spite of my faults and imperfections, one of which is that my gallbladder acts up from time to time and that I have an imperfect husband who has a 'thing' about money."

The act of verbalizing early events in our lives gives us a chance to reevaluate their significance to us. As a child, these events may have been very impressive, and we never forgot them. As an adult, we can now use our mature intelligence and experience to put these events in a more moderate perspective. This experience of past attitudes and fears in the present is called "transference." You have caught the transference and made it conscious in the present. Now you can choose to break out of it.

Vignette: Breaking the Transference

Leslie and Bill met at a party and fell head over heels in love. Their first few months together were pure enchantment, and then some of their respective mannerisms began to come out of the closet.

Leslie noticed that Bill became "upset" whenever she said "no" to one of his suggestions for the evening's activity. Bill, too, noticed that whenever he started to defend his preference for one movie over another, Leslie became agitated and very defensive.

In counseling, Leslie and Bill learned that these out-of-line reactions may have had their origins in each of their childhood pasts.

The next time Leslie became agitated, Bill was ready with a focusing question -- *"Leslie, where does that come from?"* He had caught her in the act, while she was still in the throes of a transference from the past. She coughed-up the answer immediately. When my father got angry and raised his voice, I knew I was in for a beating that would leave me half-conscious on my bedroom rug. Now when you raise your voice, it's just like the bad old days and I can't take it."

Having identified the origin of her defensiveness, Leslie was able to begin breaking the connection between Bill and her father, and between her six-year-old self and her adult self in the present.

Managing Anger

The next time Bill overreacted to Leslie's "no," she turned the tables on him. *"Where does that come from?"* she asked. "When my father said no, it was like a red flag. He was trying to control me. It didn't make any difference what I wanted to do, he'd just say 'no.' I couldn't rebel against him. It wasn't permitted. I didn't break loose from him until I was 26 years old. Now, when you say, no, I feel like you are trying to control me too, and it makes me very angry."

Leslie and Bill are still catching themselves in these transferences, but they are no longer being defeated by them. These attacks from the past are coming farther and farther apart. They are not dependent children anymore. They are independent adults with minds of their own. They are not out of control.

#91. THE WRONG QUESTION

Why Did I Let It Happen?

There are two kinds of questions, the right kind and the wrong kind. The right kind of question leads to a resolution of the problem; the wrong kind leads to a dead end and makes things worse. One such wrong question is, "What am I doing wrong?" If you knew what you were doing wrong, you wouldn't be doing it. This is our old feeling of inadequacy to cope coming to the fore. We are condemning ourself without even knowing what we have done. It isn't right or wrong, it is merely imperfect and inappropriate. We can now use our adult judgment to find out what reality requires us to do, so that we can do it. We are worthwhile human beings in the meantime.

Another example of a "wrong" question is, "Why did I let it happen?" This question implies that we are specifically guilty of the crime of "failing to prevent it." In addition, it implies that we are responsible for preventing bad things from happening, and when they do, we are guilty of the crime of irresponsibility.

240

These mistakes are based in turn on our mistaken definition of "control." We have learned as a child that "bad things happen when I lose control." To five year olds, it appears reasonable to conclude that they can keep themselves from being hurt by preventing these bad things from happening. They appoint themselves the sole responsibility for doing so. When something bad happens, they have no one but themselves to blame, they "let it happen." If they only knew why, they could tighten up the controls and prevent it from happening again next time. They are seeking to improve their technique, if you will. In the meantime, they are feeling victimized by this "bad thing," and they compound their distress by faulting their strategic defense system. They are blaming the victim -- themselves.

It is all a childhood misperception that should have been outgrown but was not. It is a mistake to define control as preventing bad things from happening. It is a useless good intention that we have for ourselves. We are so busy controlling in this absurd and inappropriate way that we are, in effect, out of control in the real world.

It is nonsense because in an imperfect world bad things happen every fifteen minutes. They cannot be prevented by standing sentry duty at the front door. That is not living, that is preventing, and it is a full-time job. We had put ourselves on guard duty twenty years ago and forgotten to take ourselves off.

Self-respecting people do not make these mistakes. They take reasonable, realistic precautions, of course, but they do not devote their lifetimes to such negative, life-destroying ambitions as preventing bad things from happening. They take the ups and downs of life as they come and do the best they can with them. They do not imagine that they have the power to prevent a child from skinning his knee or a spouse from falling ill. Their worth as a person is not at stake, so they do not take these misfortunes personally at all. These events are regrettable, but they didn't let them happen. They had no power to prevent it in the first place.

Vignette: I Should Have Known

Tina was having anxiety attacks in the morning. They started two years ago. *"What happened two years ago?"* "Nothing much. . . . Oh yes, I remember, I was raped."

Tina's morning anxiety can be understood as anger that has been mismanaged and turned into a symptom. Tina was aware of her terrible anger at the rapist and at her boyfriend who failed utterly to cope with her crisis. She had worked through these angers with a rape counselor.

She had not, however, worked through her anger at herself.

"I must have been stupid to go out jogging so late. I should have known better. It's like I let it happen." This anger at herself was below the level of conscious awareness. It was beyond her control. Her out-of-control anger was making her feel that she was out of control, that something else terrible was going to happen, and she couldn't prevent that, either. That feeling manifested itself as anxiety.

Tina learned the fallacy of blaming herself for her own victimization. It was not her fault at all, and she is guilty of nothing. She merely used a public area for her own purposes as is her right under the Constitution. She is not stupid for not knowing the future in advance. She is not guilty for failing to prevent it from happening.

Tina understood all of this intellectually, but she didn't integrate it emotionally until she remembered meeting a woman at her group who had been raped in her own kitchen. She didn't "let it happen" at all! She was minding her own business at the time and still it happened. She was able to put this issue of "letting" into a more realistic, regrettable perspective. "Letting" has nothing to do with it.

"You cannot build yourself up by tearing others down."

Rudolph Dreikurs

Tina had been displacing her many angers onto her boyfriend, who, of course, made the mistake of taking her anger personally and feeling compelled to defend his integrity. Tina hated these fights and blamed herself for "letting them happen" when she should have had enough insight by now to prevent them.

Tina was "shoulding" on herself. In so doing, she was setting herself up for more guilt, self-recrimination and self-anger.

Tina is learning to see that there is no such "should." Should is merely a preference. True, it would be preferable if she were strong enough in herself to catch herself about to displace her anger on Brad and choose not to. With practice someday she will. In the meantime, she is a worthwhile human being in spite of these imperfections. As she does her homework day by day and validates her worth as a person, these regrettable lapses will come farther apart and, one day, cease. She is learning that these negative things happen to imperfect people in an imperfect world and that she can replace her inappropriate feelings of guilt with appropriate feelings of regret when they do, but "letting" is not the problem and it does not have to be solved.

#92. YELLING AND SCREAMING

The "Yelling and Screaming" technique is quite popular with parents of younger children, older children and middle-aged children. This technique is not successful in the long run because it teaches the children to yell and scream back; this is how anger is managed and problems are solved in their house.

This is not a terribly sophisticated technique because it requires absolutely no brains. It is not a civilized technique; in fact, it is a decivilizing technique. It does not make the children better, only worse. They learn nothing from screaming except that their parents are out of control. Children resent their parent's unfair abuse of their power. When we scream our anger at a fellow human being, it is an indication that we do not know what else to do. It is a declaration of emotional bankruptcy.

For many parents, teachers, bosses, politicians and others, screaming seems to be a short cut to solving problems. It's a great little time saver. Instead of taking the time to express their legitimate anger appropriately like grown-up ladies and gentlemen, they scream it out. It's easier that way. Some day they will learn what many of us already know -- that it is easier to do it the hard way.

The Nonscreamers

Some of us never learned the "Yelling and Screaming" technique from our anger illiterate parents. We were not allowed to express any anger at all, let alone yell and scream. We learned that we would be beaten and shunned if we broke the code of silence. We learned that children who express anger outwardly are unlovable and worthless. Under these circumstances, the expression of anger was a luxury that we could not afford. Some of us have had to acquire the "Yelling and Screaming" technique in later life.

Vignette: An All-Time First

As a child, Ivy was not allowed to scream. She had health problems, and screaming was considered to be dangerously stressful for her. One day when her dolly's head fell off, she yelled and screamed her impotent rage. Daddy beat her with a belt in order to discourage this stressful behavior in the future. This was his good intention.

Ivy learned her lesson well. Now she does not express anger or any other emotion. Her fear is that if she expresses any emotion, even a happy one, the dam will burst and she will get another beating. She imagines that she is "controlling" her anger in a mature, appropriate way. However, she learned this technique of suppressing her anger when she was four years old. There is nothing mature or appropriate about it.

After some period of counselling, Ivy's homework was to write her anger down in the form of an anger letter to her misguided father and her copeless, hand-wringing mother. It took a while, but she managed to do it. It took more courage than she thought she had, but she worked up to it over time.

This accomplishment prepared her for an even more radical break with her tormented past. Her next homework was to express her anger openly. She was able to do her anger homework the following week. Her friend, Annie, canceled a dinner date at the last minute. Instead of swallowing her anger, as she usually did, she had the courage now to tell the truth. *"It makes me angry when you stand me up. What am I supposed to do now? I am very disappointed in you, Annie. That hurts my feelings."* Anne apologized, which she had never done before. Moreover, she arranged to make it up to Ivy by taking her out to dinner Sunday night. Ivy felt validated and vindicated. She had affirmed herself as a person in the world. This was not "aggressiveness" or "bitchiness" -- it was appropriate responsibility for her own sanity.

Soon afterwards, life presented Ivy with another opportunity to do some homework on a still higher plateau. Ivy worked in a flower shop. She delivered an order for a bouquet to Mrs. Preston, an old and difficult customer. As usual, Mrs. Preston refused to pay the thirty dollars on the bill. "Here's ten dollars. Take it or leave it." Ivy had a difficult decision to make. She was angry at Mrs. Preston for putting her in this ridiculous position of having to haggle on the front porch over a measly twenty bucks.

All of a sudden, Ivy let loose! She yelled and screamed at Mrs. Preston, using words that she had never been allowed to use, not even in her dreams. She yelled and yelled. Mrs. Preston's jaw dropped, but she said nothing. After she was through yelling and screaming, Ivy grabbed the ten dollar bill and drove back to the shop. She poured out her story to her boss, Harry, who had been through this many times. He could take it, but it made him angry that this nonrational person was taking her pain out on a vulnerable shop assistant. He called her up and told her to come over with the twenty dollars, which she did.

In the meantime, Ivy was evaluating her strange performance on the front porch. For the first time in her life, she let her anger out in this unseemly, "out-of-control" way. Yet she was not out of control, she was angry. She let her anger happen, and when she was through, she stopped. She was not paralyzed with fear of what the neighbors or her parents would think if they found out. She was not paralyzed by fear of displeasing people who were not afraid to displease her. She felt good. In fact, she felt triumphant. She had vented her anger and lived. She felt all the facets of self-respect including: identity, maturity, appropriate responsibility, liberation, independence, equality, security and even trust in her judgment. She hadn't lived on Mrs. Preston's absurd terms, but on her own imperfect but valid terms. She had a feeling of accomplishment, success and confidence that she could do it again.

For the first time, she had the power of choice. The yelling and screaming option had never been open to her before. Now it was. It was her right and her responsibility to use this choice constructively and not destructively. She had the adult judgment now to tell her where and when this technique was appropriate. When it was not, she still had other choices to fall back on. She could tell the truth, write an anger letter, walk away or give it a pass. She was not her father's daughter anymore -- she was Ivy's Ivy.

#93. ZIEBARTING YOUR BRAINS

When you buy a new car, they tell you to protect the undercarriage so that salt and moisture will not get in through the cracks and rust your car out from the inside.

The mischief makers in your life are a lot like road salt. They are corrosive, persistent and merciless. They will seek out your weak spots and infiltrate your life. They will use your vulnerabilities against you and destroy you from within. They will do it all without even being aware that they are doing it. Maybe you need to undercoat your brains so that these people cannot eat you up alive with their nonsense. We call this undercoating process, "Disengaging from the Mischief." It begins with the awareness that the other person is doing something that doesn't need to be done, such as criticizing, judging, condemning, ordering, manipulating, intimidating and so on. The person is throwing up a smoke screen to knock you off balance and provoking you to make countermischief that you would not be making if he or she would leave you alone.

Once you have identified people's negative behavior as nonsensical mischief, "It's only kid stuff," you can begin the process of taking away from them the power to make you crazy, bring you down to their level or make you do things you don't want to do. You can do this by correcting your two fatal mistakes.

The Two Fatal Mistakes

1. You can learn not to take mischief personally, as if it were a reflection on your worth as a person. For instance, if three-year- old Josh says, "I don't love you," we do not take his little jab, painful though it might be, at face value, as if he really meant it and were making sense. He is not making sense and is merely making mischief in order to accomplish some post-toddler purpose of his own, such as getting revenge on you for not giving him a

ZIEBARTING YOUR BRAINS

fourth cookie. It is not a reflection on your parenting skills or on your worth as a human being. If you take it personally, you will overreact nonrationally and you will try to pound him back into loving you as he apparently did just yesterday. It is important that you understand that this is how mischief makers try to solve their problems at our expense. It doesn't work, of course, but it is all they know. You can teach them better solutions to the problems of living together, but not if you have already made the mistake of taking their nonsense to heart. Your antidote against doing so is your self-respect. You need not make the mistake of defining your personal worth in terms of your child's love in the first place. You are a worthwhile human being in spite of your faults and imperfections. Whether Josh loves you or not in the second place, he loves you in the third place.

2. You can learn not to take their mischief literally, as if it made sense or was even intended to make sense. Sense has nothing to do with it. These people are not making mischief with their higher cognitive powers. They are reacting to the pain of their unsolved life problems. Their negative behavior arises from their nonrational attitudes. You must not debate the validity of their mischief, as if it were worthy of serious consideration and rebuttal.

Disengaging from the mischief means catching yourself about to make these two mistakes and choosing consciously and deliberately not to. Having so chosen, you are now free to respond on your own terms instead of merely reacting to theirs. They are no longer in control of you -- you are.

"There are no rights without responsibilities."

Rudolph Dreikurs

APPENDIX A - ANGER LETTERS

An Anger Letter To A Dead Husband

Dear George:

How dare you die on me and leave me without an identity. I had a role as Mrs. George Drago and now to this day I still do not have an identity. My brothers never allowed me a role. I'm angry and am suffering with the following diagnosed symptoms due to your death:

1. spastic colon and uncontrollable bowel

2. hiatal hernia

3. diverticulitis

4. hypertension of the bowel

5. ulcer

The hiatal hernia leaves me with terrible pain and heart-burn that comes up to my throat. It's hard for me to get my words out. Maybe that is why. Now I can see that writing is much easier for me than talking to you without my thoughts written down. No wonder I get the flu and sore throats so often -- yet another indication of not expressing words on how I feel. There is a great fear that you left me with upon your death. I was a victim of your loss and grievance. I thought you married me for better or for worse, for a lifetime, but you died after four years and two children. You made me feel like a victim.

I hate you and am still angry at you for leaving me at the age of 33 and forcing me to stand on my own two feet and raise two small children all by myself. I was forced to build my confidence and become more self-sufficient, stronger and more responsible, which made me grow up and mature in a hurry. I no longer had a post to lean on. Most of all, I lost my feeling of belonging and security and was alone to find my place in society, I still felt I did not belong. I felt like a victim of insecurity and abandonment. As a child I was abandoned and now you abandoned me a second time. My fear is that I will be abandoned again. I have not found another relationship because of that fear.

You made me lose my self-respect. I felt like a nobody again with no identity and no longer a worthwhile human being. I was in the prime of my life. Your sisters were a thorn in my side because, while they helped me financially when the children were small, I had to account to them for every move I made. I felt like a prisoner in my own house. When your sister died, I felt freed from my prison. I went back to college to learn how to manage my money.

On the day of your funeral, your best boyfriend, Jim, told me that you took pills in the service which were as big as a half dollar, in order to dissolve your kidney stones. These kidney stones finally killed you, but I never knew how serious your problem was. This statement just devastated me -- to think that you didn't have the courage to confide in me. How could you do this to me? To this day I am still angry at you for not confiding in me and for all the suffering I am still going through with my poor health, which is due to your death thirty years ago.

You did an injustice to me by dying and today I'm still angry at you for using me and lying to me.

Anne Drago

Anne's physical health improved after relieving her years of suppressed anger.

An Anger Letter to an Alcoholic Friend

Beth and her group of friends are very close and have been good friends since high school. The five of them talk on the phone each day (frequently making use of "three-way calling") and basically are there for each other through thick and thin. Proms, weddings, in-law problems, first baby deliveries, moving days, house fires and Christmas, they were there. It was a really successful support system. Even their husbands couldn't beat them, so they joined in and became close friends themselves.

Yet all was not perfect. As we stated, the group had their problems individually and collectively, and the girls could usually see each other through and ride it out. But there was one problem that was the vexation of them all. It was insidious and getting worse as time went on. Tina had begun to drink, and slowly over the years, like a dysfunctional family, the group was starting to deteriorate. They were being involved in crisis after crisis. It was like quicksand. Like many alcoholics, Tina's behavior was often out of control and the girls would be called on to help her.

Tina was always the leader of the group. Tina was the strong one, and they all loved her. This didn't make it easier for them to cope with her negative behavior. Beth had even moved in with Tina and her mother when, as a teenager, Beth and her mother weren't getting along. Beth felt she owed Tina and her family a lot. Yet, Beth and the other girls were finding it harder and harder to ignore Tina's behavior. Her neglect of her children, verbally abusive phone calls and frequent trips to the emergency room were becoming just too stressful.

To confuse the issue further, Tina was in denial. No one could even mention her drinking or Tina would fly off the handle and wreak havoc with counterattacks and other mischief.

Beth and the others truly loved Tina. They were worried about her and wanted desperately not to lose her friendship. Even though Tina was very protective of her drinking, the girls knew that by being quiet and pretending it wasn't there (as Tina preferred), they were only enabling her to continue this destructive lifestyle. They did not know what else to do. They felt trapped and powerless.

Finally, Tina caught wind of some talk about her "condition." She went out of control, accused them of mutiny, of being malicious behind her back and blamed Beth for being the instigator. Tina further responded by telling tales on each one of them, some true, some not true. It didn't matter to Tina what she said as long as they started turning against each other and took the heat off her. She had created a smoke screen and for awhile it worked.

One day Beth couldn't take it anymore and came to the Anger Clinic. She was hurt and confused. Where had all the love and support gone? Fifteen years of friendships were being shot to hell. She didn't know what to do. It was such a mess. Shortly into therapy, Beth was advised to write an anger letter to Tina. It was suggested that she use an ancient technique called "Telling The Truth."

Here is Beth's letter. Notice how Beth took her therapist's advice and:

1. Kept it simple

2. Told the truth

3. Came from a position of love and respect

4. Spoke only for herself. She did not confuse the issue by speaking for three other people

5. Stuck to the main point and addressed only the main issues.

Beth decided that the main issues that she needed to address were as follows:

1. that she truly cares for Tina and values their fifteen year friendship;

2. that she (Tina) has a drinking problem;

3. the fact that she (Tina) needs help;

4. that Beth will no longer accept Tina's drunken behavior. In the future she will not expose herself or her children to Tina when she has had too much to drink.

Here is Beth's anger letter:

Dear Tina:

I am writing this letter because I love you and care for you very much. We've been friends for half of our lives and that's saying an awful lot. There aren't many people who can say that they've had friendships last so long. I am really angry and hurt that you would think that I would ever maliciously hurt you in any way. What I am doing right now is not talking to you while you are drunk.

The last time you called me you were drunk and I will not talk to you when you're in that condition. I never said I wouldn't talk to you at all. As a matter of fact I said, "Call me when you are sober."

Tina, you have a drinking problem. You have had a drinking problem for quite some time. This is not the first time you've had this problem and if you don't get some help it will destroy you. Yes, Tina, you need some help. I know that you are probably in shock right now because I have never come out and said this so blatantly before.

I have asked myself why the "A" word, "Alcoholic," has always been so taboo. Why was alcoholism a "sensitive" subject-- your "trigger" spot? There is only one answer and that is that deep down inside you know you are an alcoholic. This wasn't a problem for you when we were in high school or even the beginning of college, but it became a problem later on. I have tried to figure it out and I think it was after you and Steve broke up. Actually, I can remember the first time you got angry with me for talking to Jeff about your drinking problem. That made me angry, but I never had the courage to tell you. I am telling you now. I am angry at you for what you are doing to my friend, Tina. You are killing her and depriving me of someone who used to make me happy. I am angry about the loss. I am hoping that my anger will get through to you so that you will start to take my concern seriously.

Anyway, my point is that you have a problem with your drinking. Even though you told me not to worry when we talked about this a few weeks ago, I am worried and I will continue to worry about you because I do love you and care for you. I know you've got your share of problems. So do I, but I do feel that you don't value our friendship. Tina, there is no conspiracy. I am not trying to hurt you. I am only trying to help you. That is what friends are for. You may not need or want my help, but I am your friend. I do care and I am sincerely worried.

You know, we've been estranged, in a way, for the last year and a half. Part of the reason is because after you gave birth to Tommy you started to drink heavily again. Because there was such a taboo on the subject, I never said anything to you or to anyone else until recently. It has taken me a long time to finally confront you. It has always been difficult for me to confront you, but that is another issue that isn't important right now.

What is important is that I am confronting you whether you like it or not and I will continue to confront you as long as we maintain a friendship. Tina, I wish you could see it. I wish you could look at yourself in a magic mirror and see deep down inside. But there is no magic mirror and you're going to have to look in a mirror soon.

I wish you would stop blaming your drinking on your problems. See that your drinking is only making your problems worse and please realize that they aren't going away or changing every time you try to escape.

I have so much to say to you, so much more I want to resolve with you, but this isn't the time. I won't play tit for tat. The point of this letter is to let you know that I am here for you and I always will be. But I cannot be there for you when you are drunk. I am sorry that things aren't the way you want them to be. But I have realized that life just doesn't always go the way you plan. In life, you need to adapt and adjust. There are so many things in my life that weren't "in the plan." I have had to adjust and when I can't, I get some help.

Please, for your sake, for Jeff's sake and for Tommy's, but most importantly for your sake -- get some help. You know it's O.K. to get help. You've done it before and you can do it again. If you need me I am here for you.

Love,

Beth

Introduction To The Facets Of Self-Contempt And Self-Respect

Rudolph Dreikurs, a student of Alfred Adler, defined self-respect as "the feeling that one is a worthwhile human being in spite of one's faults and imperfections."

This definition is not expressed in terms of "knowing," but of "feeling." It is not based on objective conditions, it is a subjective experience. It is not conditional and does not depend upon external indicators of achievement. It cannot be given or taken away by external agencies.

The therapeutic process consists of replacing the client's underlying self-contempt with self-respect. This is not done by bolstering their self-esteem with pats on the back or empty shouts of encouragement. We see self-esteem as an "estimation" or opinion of oneself. If this estimation is based on false premises, parental indulgence or mistaken logic, what is it worth? It is worth nothing. People who swagger and strut do not have high self-esteem, as their admiring, naive subjects seem to believe; this is arrogance and bravado. We understand their veneer of superiority as their way of relieving the pain of their feelings of inferiority and inadequacy. They are overcompensating for their underlying convictions that they are not good enough. This is their way of keeping their secret inferiority from leaking out. They are preventing the painfully humiliating exposure of their "worthlessness."

They are not worthless -- they just feel that way and behave accordingly. This feeling of self-contempt is below the level of conscious awareness; it is an attitude that they have towards themselves. It is the task of therapy to replace this negative attitude with a positive one. This positive attitude is called self-respect.

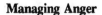

"We do not require perfection, we require improvement."

Rudolph Dreikurs

Self-contempt generalizes from individuals to their families, cultures and communities. They can not aspire to high achievement. They can only sink to the lowest common denominator of personal and group performance. Anyone who achieves success is looked on as a "show off" to be brought down to a lower level where he or she belongs. Anyone who is happy is seen as a deviation from the general atmosphere of misery and a way is found to destroy this happiness which is inconsistent with the prevailing self-hatred. Such people cannot enjoy happiness. They can only escape from their pain into negative excitement, which is always self-indulgent, counterproductive and self-destructive.

It is our belief that many social problems arise from feelings of self-contempt which predispose individuals to take without giving, to cooperate negatively instead of positively, to succeed at failing and to bring about their own destruction as well as that of their loved ones.

The antidote to this epidemic of self-contempt and self-anger is self-respect.

Self-respecting people do not have to overcompensate for anything because there is nothing to overcompensate for. They do not have to anaesthetize the pain of their existence because it isn't there. They feel good enough as they are. This is not a prescription for stagnation, but an invitation to do as much with their lives as they can and to make a positive contribution to their community instead of a negative one. They are not dependent on others for the validation of their contribution, they are capable of validating their own accomplishments. They do not have to live on other people's terms because they have independent, valid terms of their own. They are free to live their lives in cooperation with their fellow human beings as equals.

The goal of psychotherapy is often expressed as the relief from anxiety or depression through the attainment of security ("I feel so vulnerable"); identity ("I don't know who I am"); decisiveness ("I can't make up my mind"); or control ("I can't stop eating"). As we will see from the following list of facets, these positive qualities do not exist as entities in themselves, they are all components of self-respect. When the primary goal of replacing self-contempt with self-respect is achieved, all of these secondary goals are achieved at the same time.

APPENDIX B - THE FACETS OF SELF-CONTEMPT

Self-contempt is a complex emotion consisting of the following feelings and emotions:

1. Feelings of Pressure, Tension and Stress:

a) Feelings of pressure arise from our attempts to live on other people's terms, especially when we don't know what those terms are. Examples of such pressure include our need to please others, and to live up to externally imposed standards and ideals, to be responsible and never irresponsible, to avoid displeasing others by failing to live up to their expectations, to control others so that nothing bad will happen, to control life for the same reason and to be right and never wrong.

Anger creates a pressure of its own. It threatens to reveal the underlying fraudulence of our "pleasingness" and "super-responsibility," which are merely overcompensatory roles that we have been playing since childhood. We respond to the pressure of this threat with counterpressure for the purpose of stuffing our anger back down where it can't do us any harm.

b) Tension is often created when there is a gap between the demands of reality and our feelings of inadequacy to cope with those demands. Tension arises out of not knowing what we "should" know. For example, our tension at a party may arise from our perceived need to do the proper thing and our equally perceived ignorance as to what the proper thing might be. The tension is compounded by our striving to prevent the humiliating exposure of our ignorance on these occasions. Tension also arises when we try to prevent disasters from happening in the future without knowing what the disaster is, nor when it will happen.

c) Stresses include trying to maintain a facade of self-confidence and success in order to keep people from finding out how insecure we feel inside, trying to keep up external appearances when our internal realities are in despair and trying to be happy while suffering from the conviction that we do not deserve to be happy. Stress arises from striving to be better than we are when we do not know what "better" means or how to achieve it. Stress arises from the pain of our existence or self-contempt, and from our striving to relieve that pain in ways that do not work.

2. Feeling out of Control: In our self-contempt, we feel that we do not deserve happiness and success. We feel unworthy. All we deserve is unhappiness and failure, and that is all we have to look forward to. We proceed to prophesy a lifetime of unhappiness and failure for ourselves. We predict disaster.

Unhappiness and failure are very painful. As part of our self-contempt, we have a tendency to exaggerate the pain of these eventualities. At the same time we underestimate our ability to tolerate the pain. The prospect of disaster becomes overwhelming. We cannot cope with ordinary disappointments of life under these circumstances. Our only hope is to control our existence in order to prevent these bad things from happening. That way, we won't have to cope with them. We soon find that we cannot prevent bad things from happening in an imperfect world. We are the prisoner of our mistaken definition of control, and, as a consequence, we feel out of control most of the time.

3. Lack of Identity: When we do not respect ourselves, we tend to play roles as an adult that we acquired in childhood. In the absence of a well formed adult identity of our own, we tend to live our life on other people's terms -- that is, we avoid displeasing people, we try to live up (or down) to their expectations of us, their preferences become our preferences, their judgment is our judgment and their scenario is our scenario.

4. Feelings of Immaturity: When we carry childhood attitudes and convictions about ourselves into adulthood such as "I am a victim," we understandably feel less mature than we would otherwise. We compare ourselves unfavorably to the more competent, self-confident adults around us. We may feel faintly ridiculous and we fear that our "ridiculousness" will be found out. We may feel that we will grow up someday in the indeterminate future, perhaps after we get our Master's Degree only to find that a master's degree is no guarantee of maturity, either.

5. Feeling of Not Belonging -- Anomie: Many of us feel that we do not deserve to belong. We may also feel that we do not know how to belong and therefore, we cannot ever come to belong. Our problem seems insoluble. This "insolubility" is a contributing factor in our depression and loneliness.

We may seek to relieve the pain of our nonbelonging by becoming a joiner, only to find that we have contempt for any organization that would have us. We drop out, feeling worse off than we did before. The "Joiner" is a role like all others -- the Victim, the Rebel and the Pleaser. We cannot relieve the pain of our "outcast" feeling by replacing one role with another. Even the Crown Prince role that is played by the spoiled brat who seems so superior to everyone else fails to assuage the pain of not belonging. The Crown Prince has "solved" this problem by turning it upside down and says, "I don't have to belong to them, they have to belong to me, and I won't let them! I belong and they don't."

We may have the feeling that we do not belong in our marriage, in our home, in our work unit. We may think something like, "The boss's pet belongs, but I don't." Teenagers who do not respect themselves may find a group of nonbelongers like themselves and form a gang. Together, they will make useless, destructive mischief which will give the participants a feeling of negative belonging, which to them is better than no belonging at all.

Our feeling of not belonging predisposes us to play certain peripheral roles, such as The Spectator or The Passive Observer of the Passing Scene. Some of us have the feeling that we are in limbo or that we are waiting for our life to begin.

6. Feelings of Insecurity: One concomitant of the feeling of self-contempt is the feeling that we are insecure, unsure and vulnerable to the painful vicissitudes of life. We doubt our capacity to defend ourselves successfully. In the absence of an internal sense of personal security against the ups and downs of everyday life, we buy extra locks for the doors. We try to make our life predictable and we look for ways to exempt ourselves from the pain of failure by not trying in the first place.

7. Distrust: People who don't respect themselves have trouble trusting others. They may have seen their parents betraying each other's trust or they may have a personal recollection of a painful betrayal by someone they loved and trusted. They may have concluded that they can prevent the pain of future betrayals by trusting no one. For them, there is no middle ground between total trust and total distrust.

Because they cannot trust their own judgment, they often find themselves making the double error of not trusting those they should trust and trusting those that they should not.

8. Feelings of Inequality: When we are small, we compare ourselves unfavorably to our older siblings, cousins and playmates. In our naive system of measurement, older is more desirable and younger is less desirable. Bigger is better and little is worthless. We define our personal worth in these simplistic terms. The trouble is that some of us never outgrow it. Even as adults, we are sensitive to these hierarchies of who is better and who is worse, as if these rankings determined our worth to ourselves.

We also compare our group to other groups -- whether it is our family, work group or bowling team. When we feel unequal, we may feel that our group is unequal. We resent the unfairness of this ranking whether it is deserved or not. What prevents us from changing bowling teams? We do not "deserve" to belong to a winning team. We might fail. Our inferiorities might be exposed. No, it is safer to remain loyal to the Chickadees than risk everything by transferring to the Bluebirds.

What prevents us from making a new friend? If the new friend is more popular than we are, we will find a way to put them off. We may fail to return phone calls or we "forget" a date. The friend drops us and looks elsewhere. Our self-contempt predisposes us to behave in ways that are guaranteed to maintain the consistency of our inequality, and we hate it.

9. **Feelings of Guilt:** People who have contempt for themselves tend to feel like worthless failures. They feel that they have failed to live up to the standards and expectations that have been held out for them. They don't question the validity of these unrealistically high standards -- they only know that they "aren't good enough." They compound their despair by assuming that this painful failure is their fault. It is their responsibility. They have no one but themselves to blame. They are guilty. They do not know what they are guilty of, nor how their guilt can be relieved.

In addition to these generalized guilts, the individual may be susceptible to specific guilts, such as the failure to be pleasing enough at a dinner party, responsible enough to prevent a child from being injured. Some of us feel guilty of the crime of failing to be sufficiently unselfish. For instance Rose, for the first time in her life insisted that her husband not buy a new bowling ball for Christmas. There were some things she needed for the house that would make them both happy. She knew that her priorities were right, but her old attitude from childhood would always catch up to her and prevent her from asking for what she needed. She would think, "Giving to others is good, taking is bad, i.e., selfish." This year, she learned to see her priorities in a new light. She was not taking anything away from her husband that he really needed. Instead, she was securing his cooperation in the resolution of a domestic situation for their mutual benefit. That is not selfish at all.

Edith could not allow her date to pay for her dinner. She insisted on being fair, independent, liberated and mature. Underneath these high-sounding ideals was her fear of being found guilty of the crime of selfishness. She felt that she was taking without giving. It was pointed out to her that this was not the case. She was giving her escort her time and the pleasure of her company and this was his way of reciprocating. There was no selfishness, crime or guilt -- only cooperation between two equal members of the human race.

10. **Feelings of Oppression and Slavery:** We go through life feeling inferior to others who are bigger and stronger than we are. Since we cannot afford the luxury of kindness ourselves, we cannot imagine that others can be kind. They can only be cruel and we expect them to use their superiority over us in hurtful, degrading ways. We become "Professional Oppressees," seeing oppression at every turn, even where no oppression is intended. When someone asks us to cooperate, we confuse cooperation with submission and we balk.

Since we cannot trust our own judgment because it isn't good enough, we have difficulty in solving problems and making decisions. We tend to make inappropriate choices which tend to confirm our conviction that our judgment isn't good enough. Our self-sabotage puts us at a disadvantage. Others take advantage of the opportunity that we have created for them. When they do, we tend to feel trapped, discouraged and resentful of the more effective people around us. We are not really their slave. We just do not see how our feelings of inadequacy contribute to our own distress. We cannot blame ourselves because it would hurt too much. So we must blame others for our difficulties, making our problems insoluble. We are the prisoners of our own self-doubt.

11. **Feelings of Dependency:** When we cannot trust our competence to cope with the tasks of life, we feel compelled to depend on the resources of individuals who seem to be more adequate than we are. Our "advantage" in being dependent on others is that if there is a disaster, it will be their fault, not ours. Since we are exempt from responsibility, our dependency has been converted from a liability into an asset. We can not see any advantage under these circumstances to becoming independent. It isn't worth the grief. When the other person depends on our dependency, we have co-dependency.

12. **Allergic to Accomplishment:** Unself-respecting people have no hope of accomplishing anything of significance in the world. They cannot, therefore, take the initiative in accomplishing anything useful and constructive. Even when they do accomplish a task, they are quick to pooh-pooh it. This is called "undoing."

In their despair, all they deserve is negative accomplishment. They succeed in accomplishing things that do not need to be accomplished, they make mischief. They succeed at failing. They become destructive of themselves and others. They may fail passively through inaction or actively become destroyers with no thought to what will take the place of what they have torn down.

13. **Allergic to Success:** Many of us suffer from the conviction that we "can't win for losing." We have the Reverse Midas Touch - everything we touch turns bad. Our behavior is consistent with these attitudes and we arrange to snatch defeat from the jaws of victory every time. We succeed at failure. It isn't much, but it's all we've got.

14. **Negative Success**: We arrange to succeed at failing because we are afraid to succeed at succeeding. We have the attitude: "If I succeed on Monday, they'll expect me to do it again on Tuesday. I'm not sure I can do it two days in a row, so I'd better not start anything I can't finish. Besides, who am I to succeed at succeeding? I don't deserve to. I am unworthy. I'd only feel guilty of perpetrating a fraud. They would find out how undeserving I am. It would be humiliating."

15. **Lack of Confidence**: "If I've never succeeded in the past, how can I expect to succeed in the future? My skills aren't good enough, my judgment isn't good enough. I'd only make things worse, so why try?" This is called negative confidence -- "I know I'm going to screw it up. I can count on it."

16. **Lack of Courage -- Discouragement**: "I am not willing to take the risks required to live in the real world. I might fail to be good enough and the pain would be unbearable. Everyone would know how inferior and inadequate I really am. It's not worth it. What's the use of trying. I know in advance that I am not going to succeed."

17. **Inappropriate Responsibility**: When we do not trust our competence to assume appropriate responsibility for the tasks of life, we may try to solve the responsibility problem by assuming more responsibility than the situation requires. The purpose of our inappropriate behavior is not to get the job done faster, but to prove that we are not inadequate to cope after all. We become super-responsible, which is a good intention to do more than reality requires us to do. We cannot keep it up. We will burn ourselves out in the end.

18. **Irresponsibility**: We may seek to exempt ourselves from our responsibilities by devising ingenious cover stories with which to deceive the important others in our life, as well as ourselves. For instance, "I'm not feeling well today" or "I'm just too busy." Our logic is: "The less I do, the less I'll screw up. If

I don't do it, no one will ever know how inadequate I am. Then I can't fail." We never question the validity of our prophecy that we are going to fail. It is consistent with our self-contempt.

19. **Inappropriate Anger or Suppressed Rage:** Another facet of our self-contempt is our failure to learn how to manage our anger appropriately. Instead, we have come to believe that our anger is not a legitimate human emotion. Since we are not valid, our anger cannot be valid either. Invalid anger cannot be expressed appropriately. We can only suppress it until we reach a point where we cannot suppress it any longer. When something in the present provokes us to the breaking point, we erupt all over the place. This inappropriate overreaction confirms our negative attitudes towards ourselves, our anger and the consequences of expressing it. We suppress it again and the cycle repeats itself.

20. **Distrusting Our Judgment:** Unself-respecting people have contempt for their decision-making ability. They have contempt for their judgment, which is the organ of decision making. They cannot trust any judgment as imperfect as their own. In trying to outsmart themselves -- "If I think I am right, I must be wrong" -- they make the wrong choice, thus confirming their self-contempt. Or, they make no choice at all, deferring to the "superior" judgment of others. They feel trapped, but they do not usually understand their trapped feeling in terms of their contempt for their judgment. They cannot initiate actions; they can only react to the actions of others, which requires no judgment at all.

Seymour has contempt for everything that is his, including his own judgment and ability to cope with problems. He cannot trust his judgment because it is "not good enough." He cannot trust the judgment or good faith of others since they are no better than he is. Even so, he is painfully dependent on the judgment of others and continues to ask for their advice. When he gets their advice, it is still up to him to decide whether to take it or not. He cannot make that decision either because he still doesn't trust his judgment. His dilemma is unresolvable.

21. **No Power of Choice:** When we play a role on someone else's terms, we cannot feel independent or secure. We forfeit our power of choice. All we can do is react to the other person's stimulus as they react to ours. Neither one of us is making conscious, appropriate choices in our own behalf.

We do not have free will. We can only make choices that are determined by our respective scenarios. For example, lifelong victims in a relationship with a victimizer cannot deviate from the scenario. They find themselves saying things that they know from past experience will only bring down more victimization on their head, such as, "Oh yeah! I'd like to see you try!" It would be out of character to say something like, "You scare me when you talk like that." That would be telling the truth, doing the unexpected and disengaging from the mischief. That is what an informed, self-respecting person would say. That choice is not open to someone who is playing the role of the victim.

A super-responsible child cannot say, "Do it yourself." A super self-reliant child cannot say, "Can you help me with this?" A Pleaser cannot say, "It makes me angry when you do that." These choices are not open to them.

Another impediment to making choices in the present is the power of attitudes from the past. Our attitudes predispose us to behave in certain ways. They save us the trouble of making trivial choices, such as, what to do when the telephone rings. We don't deliberate, we pick it up.

Sometimes, however, our trusty old attitudes aren't so trusty after all. They are out of sync with our present situation. They may have been appropriate thirty years ago, but they are not appropriate any more.

Frank and Maria spent years fighting over money. Frank didn't like paying the bills and he sometimes put them off too long, running up late payment charges that could have been avoided. Maria suggested that he let her pay the bills. He couldn't bring himself to let her. There was a "higher principle here," he said. "Men control the money, not women." His father had managed his money and his father before him. He could not betray their example of masculine household management. He would feel guilty. It was less painful to screw up the checkbook himself. It was the lesser misery. This was not a rational decision. The decision had been made a long time ago and never questioned.

Frank learned in counseling that he was the prisoner of these examples, roles and attitudes. They were not high principles at all, they were carryovers from the past. They were not Holy Writ; they could be questioned now, examined and replaced if the reality situation required it.

Frank chose to let go of the checkbook. When he did, he felt relief, control, maturity, liberation and independence. He had the power of choice. He was not his grandfather's grandson any more. He had an identity of his own. He was not playing the role of the "man of the house, doing his duty." He was free to cooperate and share responsibility with Maria in an atmosphere of mutual respect.

22. **Intellectual Self-Contempt:** Unself-respecting people have contempt for their intelligence. They feel that if they are not perfectly smart, they are "not smart enough." Since they do not know everything that they require themselves to know, their conviction is that they must be stupid. They may be very smart in some area of their existence, such as their work or in remembering baseball statistics, but these mental accomplishments do not affect their underlying emotional conviction that they are not smart enough. They arrange to "forget" or to make a self-destructive remark to their boss. Their "stupidity" is then confirmed.

23. **Feeling "Not Good Enough":** Unself-respecting people have a vague, generalized feeling that they are not good enough.

They do not know where they are lacking, nor how to make up the supposed deficiency. They do not know how good is good enough. They only "know" that they do not measure up to some vague standard of achievement that someone expects them to live up to. They may feel driven to prove that they are good enough in one specific way or another, only to find that such specific triumphs prove nothing at all about their general unworthiness.

24. Unfavorable Comparison: These people feel inferior to those who seem to be more self-respecting than they are. They are painfully sensitive to their inferior condition vis-a-vis their more "fortunate" fellows. They may resent their unfair advantage over them, and seek to pull them down to their drab level. Or they may spur themselves to rise above them only to find that they cannot sustain their advantage. Their self-contempt catches up with them sooner or later.

25. Confusing Cooperation with Submission: People who feel inferior cannot cooperate freely with their supposed superiors. They can only submit to them, rebel against them, or withdraw from them in discouragement. When their superiors seek to secure their cooperation, they are predisposed to hear their request as if it were a demand that they submit to "higher authority." This perceived demand makes them feel resentful, which means angry. As a result of this predisposition, they are angry most of the time.

26. Denying Reality: To people who have contempt for themselves, the real world is painful and dangerous. They feel inadequately prepared to cope with the problems of the real world. Debby deals with problems in the real world by denying that they exist. That way she is exempt from having to solve them and she cannot fail. She withdraws from reality and contents herself by solving problems that do not need to be solved such as preventing others from finding out how badly she really feels about herself. She puts on a facade of cheerfulness.,but it is only skin deep. When the facade cracks, everyone will be surprised. They will say, "I had no idea that things were so bad for her."

27. **Not Living in the Present:** For people who do not respect their ability to cope with the tasks of everyday life, one solution is to live in another tense, where nonexistent problems serve to distract them from uncomfortable reality. People who live in the past say things like, "If only I had. . . ." which conveniently exempts them from having to cope with the consequences of their choices in the present. People who live in the future suffer from the "Someday Syndrome." Their intention is to begin living some time in the future when certain fictitious requirements have been met. For instance, "Someday, after I get my divorce. . . ." or "Someday, after I get my revenge. . . ." They may spend their days trying to prevent something bad from happening in the future, as if they knew what was going to happen when.

These people are not only living outside the present tense, they are also living outside the indicative mood which has to do with things as they are. They live their lives in the subjunctive mood, which has to do with conditions contrary to fact. They live in a world of "as if," "what if," "if only" and "yes, but. . . ." The reason that these people feel out of it is that they are. They complain that they "can't feel their life." They have spent their lives arranging not to.

28. **Unapproachability:** People who feel badly about themselves do not want others to find out how inadequate and inferior they are. They put up facades of pleasingness, shyness, intimidation or self-reliance to keep people at a safe distance. They elevate themselves above others by attaining the heights of achievement or they fall into the pit of failure. In any case, no one will ever know their painful secret. Then, after years of putting up a wall around themselves, they wonder why they are lonely. They can't have it both ways.

29. **Selfishness:** Unself-respecting people tend to be selfish and self-centered -- they take without giving. For one thing, they

cannot give because they need it all themselves; they have nothing to spare for anyone else. They imagine that what they are grabbing for will relieve the pain of their existence. Since it never does, they need more of the same tomorrow. They are a bottomless pit of needs and wants. In addition, they cannot give of themselves because they have contempt for anything that is theirs to give. They anticipate that their "worthless" gift would be despised and rejected, so why bother offering it? It is much safer to take.

They are not consciously aware of their selfishness, but they are terribly conscious of the selfishness of others. They have their own self-serving definition of selfishness: "Anyone who does not give me what I want is selfish!"

30. **Lack of Social Interest:** People who do not respect their own worth as a person cannot take an appropriate interest in the well-being of their fellow humans. Since they do not feel equal to them, they can only feel superior or inferior. If they feel that others are superior to them, they cannot relate to them appropriately. They can fear them and curry favor or they can try to overthrow them so that they won't feel inferior anymore. But they cannot regard them as equal members of the human race.

Those who feel superior to people, can only have contempt for those whom they feel superior to. Sometimes their contempt for underlings is open and obvious. Some fictitiously superior people mask their contempt for inferiors by representing themselves as the compassionate, but ineffectual champions of the suffering underdogs of the world. They may even put these suffering underdogs on a pedestal, as though their suffering made them more human than those who do not suffer.

31. **Unlovability:** People who feel contempt for themselves as worthless do not believe that anyone can sincerely love them. On the one hand, they predict a miserable, loveless existence for themselves. On the other, they defeat all attempts on the part of potential love partners to love them and make them happy. In their

self-contempt, they can only have contempt for anyone so foolish as to love them. They cannot love such a person. They can only admire those persons who are perceptive enough to spurn them.

"Unlovable" people invest much of their time and energy defending themselves against the conviction that they are unlovable. They may downplay the importance of love in their lives or escape into fantasies of super lovability. Some of them form their own religion which requires its adherents to "love their master." They make themselves hateful to the opposite sex so that when they leave they can say, "I told you so, I knew you couldn't love me." They may blame the opposite sex for its inability or unwillingness to love them, and then become very angry at the whole gender. They may perceive individual members of that unloving gender as worthy victims of their righteous indignation. They may feel entitled to punish representatives of that gender severely for their "cruelty".

These people are not really unlovable. They are merely the prisoner of their conviction that they are. They are doomed to bring about the fulfillment of their prophecies of love and disaster forever.

Ted felt unlovable all of his life. In college, he was attractive and popular. He thought that he didn't have a problem. One night, on a date, he started to become sexually-aroused. He made an aggressive attack on Sheila, who repulsed his advances. This rejection triggered his old feeling that he was unlovable. He could not stand the pain of that confirmation. He forced himself on Sheila, not out of love or sexual tension, but to prevent the confirmation of his conviction that he is as unlovable now as he was in the playpen. He was convicted of date rape. Sheila might have loved him in time. He has seen to it that she never will. He still doesn't know "what got into" him.

32. **Out of Touch with Reality:** People who hold themselves in contempt are out of touch with the reality of their fundamental worth as human beings. They cannot be in touch with the rest of reality. Their perception and understanding of the real world will be distorted by the prism of their self-pain. They will be in touch with their overcompensatory needs, wants and strivings or with their fantasies about reality, and they will behave accordingly. They will operate on the basis of their mistaken attitudes about reality, people and about themselves.

They may be "super-intelligent," but the effective use of their intelligence will be impeded by their underlying misconceptions about their place in the world. They may suffer from the delusion that they are rational and conjure up impressive philosophical theories to explain the social, economic or political aspects of human existence. But all such products of their intelligence will be skewed by the undiscovered and unresolved doubts as to their own worthiness to be a happy, successful human being. Their generalizations about suffering mankind will stem, to a greater or lesser degree, from the particulars of their own painful introduction to life on this planet. Their remedies for relieving the pain and suffering of others will have a strong connection with the relief of their own. For instance, if their parents were poor, they may feel that the problem is poverty, and that the solution is to give everybody money. If their parents had too much money, they may feel that human problems can be solved by taking money from those who have it and giving it to those who don't. They have mistaken sameness for equality. Their ideals may seem lofty, but they are mere overcompensations for their own inability to see reality as it is.

33. **Intolerance of Pain:** Unself-respecting people are more vulnerable to pain than they need to be. They perceive the pain as a "confirmation" of their worthlessness. They feel that worthless, unsuccessful people like themselves deserve to suffer, and they see to it that they do. They mistakenly perceive pain as a victimization even where no victimization is intended. They prophesize a life of

pain for themselves and then proceed to erect pseudo-logical defenses against it. When these fictitious defenses and overcompensations fail, they blame others, which does not help, or they blame themselves, which is worse.

They do not respond to pain in ways that are appropriate. They respond in counterproductive, nonrational ways that prevent them from getting the relief that they might have been able to get otherwise.

34. Negative Compatibility: These unself-respecting people often gravitate towards each other and get married or form business partnerships. They find that they have recreated relationships that they remember from their childhood, such as Victim and Victimizer, Crown Prince and Scullery Maid, Big Sister and Baby Brother, Sparring Partners or Pleaser and Pleasee. Neither partner has enough self-respect to break the mold and put the relationship on a more appropriate basis, such as mutual respect, equality and shared responsibility.

For example, a woman who was abused by her father and brother will not be compatible with a man who is prepared to cooperate with her as an equal. She will feel uncomfortable in such a relationship and soon end it. She will not question the nature of her discomfort, nor seek to relieve it. She will persevere until she meets someone at a dance that she feels comfortable with. She has no way of knowing in advance that two years into the future he will be pulling her around by her hair just as her father did.

It is uncanny how these people find each other and then proceed to bring out the worst in each other. We do not know how they are able to penetrate the screen of "best foot forward" and link up with the destructive child behind the facade. Perhaps it is empathy that is working here which is a little known aspect of the human condition. It is little known because it is unscientific. It cannot be reproduced under laboratory conditions or at least it hasn't been so far.

Perhaps a woman who is compatible with victimizers like her father can sense the pattern of "vibration" that a charming brute radiates. Perhaps there is a constellation of vibrations that she homes in on, like a homing pigeon. In any case, we know that the process of negative attraction is not rational or logical. We ask ourselves, "What does she see in him?" If we ask her, she will come up with some cover story like, "He is so strong, so sure of himself." It is exactly these qualities that will break her cheekbone in three years and drive her to a women's shelter in four.

It is the task of the counselor to identify these negative predispositions and change them. The change is not accomplished by a direct frontal assault on the subject's dating patterns. It is done by replacing her self-contempt from childhood with self-respect in the present. Her taste in men will change accordingly. She will not be negatively compatible, she will be positively compatible with men who respect themselves. Her discomfort will have disappeared.

35. **Fear and Anxiety:** Unself-respecting people live in fear. Many of their fears have a specific object such as failing the mid-term, failing to close a deal or failing to get a date for the prom. These specific fears often exist in an aura of anxiety, which is objectless and free floating. These are some of the factors that contribute to the anxiety:

a) Anger out of control. When our anger is out of control, we are out of control. We feel like something terrible could happen to us.

b) Living in the future. When we feel inadequate to cope, we predict disaster ahead. We scare ourselves in advance.

c) Living on other people's terms. When we play a role opposite someone else's role, we make our lives unpredictable. We are dependent on the other person who is just as dependent on us.

d) Out of control. When we define control in ways that do not work, we cannot be in control of our lives. When we try harder to control in the wrong ways, we make things even worse. Something terrible is going to happen and we can't prevent it. That's scary.

e) Insecurity. When we define security in childish ways, we create problems that we do not know how to solve. We feel exposed, vulnerable and threatened. We feel unable to protect ourselves. We try to protect ourselves in ways that do not work, such as money, guns, electrified fences and dobermans, only to find that our insecurity comes right back.

f) Fictitious guilt. We suffer from fictitious guilt. We may have said something displeasing to the neighbor's mother-in-law, failed to prevent something from happening or failed to be perfectly responsible. We are afraid that our "guilts" will be uncovered and we will be sent to our room forever.

g) Real guilt. We really did do something terrible to our little sister. We live in fear of being found out. This painful fear is our punishment and that is what guilty people deserve. We would rather punish ourselves than let someone else do it. It hurts less this way.

h) Fear of change. As unhappy as we are, we are afraid to change. In our pessimism, we cannot imagine that the change will be for the better, only for the worse. We are afraid to break the continuity of our existence.

We wouldn't know who we were. We prefer the lesser misery of staying the way we are to the even worse misery of being annihilated.

i) Fear of abandonment. We may have felt abandoned by a loved one in childhood. We may have felt terrified that we would never see them again or that we would die of heartbreak and neglect. We are afraid that it will happen again. Our priority is to prevent it.

Even the thought of being abandoned makes us angry. We feel powerless to prevent the "impending" loss. We are angry at ourselves for being so vulnerable. All of these angers turn into anxiety, which compounds our original fear of being abandoned.

j) Fear of betrayal. Betrayal hurts. When we trust our little friend with our favorite toys and then find that they are missing the next day, we become very angry. We become angry with ourselves for being so trusting and so "good for nothing." We resolve not to trust again. That way, we will never be betrayed.

k) Fear of ridicule. Failure is embarrassing. Since that is all we can predict for ourselves, it is only a matter of time before we are exposed to the whole community. We will be ridiculed for our failure and for our absurd attempt to make people think that we were just like them.

l) Fear of criticism. In order to prove that we are not worthless, we strive for perfection. A criticism points out that we have missed our goal of perfection. Our goal now is to do even better next time so that no one will criticize us. There is no middle ground between perfect and worthless.

m) Fear of being wrong. As a child, there was no middle ground between right and wrong. Wrongness was punished severely. We had no hope of being right; our prayer was to be not wrong. Since we can never be perfectly right, we are doomed to be wrong forever. It is only a matter of time until our wrongness is exposed and we will be punished. We cannot stand the suspense. We confess our "wrongdoing" and ruin a relationship that does not need to be ruined.

n) Fear of anger. We feel inadequately prepared to cope with our anger situation. Some of us are afraid that we will lose control and kill somebody. Some are afraid that if we express anger, we will be punished, victimized, abandoned or annihilated. We are afraid of other people's anger. We walk on eggs to avoid provoking them.

These fears are scary enough, but there is something more. We are afraid that if any of these scary eventualities come to pass, we will ultimately be annihilated. We will die of shame or grief. We will cease to exist. On a still deeper level, the terror will not end with our death, which is bad enough, but for unself-respecting people, death is not just the end of them, death is the end of the world!

36. **Vulnerable to Temptation:** Unself-respecting people are in a lot of pain. They imagine that they can relieve their pain by escaping into negative excitement. They are vulnerable to making exciting, self-destructive mischief. They are not dissuaded by the danger, even deadly danger. If they die, that is what "worthless" people deserve anyway. Their pain will end forever. In the meantime, they are numbing out the pain of their self-contempt by engaging in "forbidden" behaviors.

37. **Internal Conflict:** Unself-respecting people hold themselves in contempt. They despise their "stupidity," "weakness" and inadequacy to cope. They hate the roles that they have learned to play -- the Pleaser, the Victim, the Good-For-Nothing. They wish that they could escape from the pain of their self-hatred but they do not know how. They carry it with them wherever they go. They cannot be at peace with others because they are not at peace with themselves. The stakes are higher than they consciously know. They must redouble their striving to prevent these disasters from happening. The "fate of mankind" hangs in the balance. This is "ultimate control" and the ultimate absurdity.

These are just a few of the facets of self-contempt. The infinite number of possible combinations and permutations of these facets, in their various strengths and degrees, accounts for the endless variety in what we call the human personality. The individual may not be consciously aware of these facets as such. They are attached to the mistaken ideas they acquired about themselves as a child, such as, "I'm not good enough" or "People are out to victimize me." These ideas are no longer conscious either, but they carry a load of negative emotional freight with them. These ideas, and their associated emotional connotations, predispose the individual to think, feel and behave in certain ways as an adult. For example, Steve is a manager. When he is required to make an adult business decision, his judgment will be colored by carryover attitudes from the past that are irrelevant and inappropriate in the present. He may, as a result, decide not to discipline an employee who deserves it because, "He won't like me anymore." He will overcompensate for his feelings of self-contempt by giving the employee a "pass." Since overcompensation is always counterproductive, the employee who knows he deserves to be disciplined, will like and respect the manager even less and behave accordingly.

Our purpose in drawing up this lengthy "laundry list" is to show how multifaceted the problem of self-contempt really is and how it underlies so many of the "problems" that we have been focusing our attention on for all these years.

We also hope that we have shown that all of these facets are interrelated, which means that a problem such as insecurity, indecision or loneliness is not the issue in and of itself. It is part of a larger issue further down. We also wish to make it clear that, as we gradually replace our underlying self-contempt with self-respect, the presenting problem, as well as the other facets which may not have been as apparent, are all relieved and replaced by the corresponding facet of self-respect at the same time.

APPENDIX C - THE FACETS OF SELF-RESPECT

Self-respect is a complex emotion consisting of the following feelings and emotions keyed to facets of self-contempt.

1. **Relief**: People who learn how to replace their self-doubt with self-respect experience a feeling of relief from tension, stress and pressure. This feeling includes relief from the pressures of having to prove that one is not worthless, to succeeding, to avoiding displeasing others and preventing bad things from happening; relief from the tensions that arise when one's perceptions about reality are not congruent with the real world; relief from the stress of maintaining a facade of self-confidence and success in order to conceal ones underlying feeling of worthlessness and inadequacy.

2. **Control:** People who respect themselves feel that although they are not perfectly in control of their situation, they feel able to function in the real world. They do not define control in terms of controlling others, life or their emotions -- all of which would only set them up to fail and feel even more out of control. They do not define control in terms of preventing bad things from happening. Instead, they define control as making things happen, which includes the ability to make things not happen, and taking life as it comes and doing the best they can with it. Positive control is predicated on the trust in their judgment as to what the reality of the situation requires them to do and the courage do it.

3. **Identity:** Self-respecting people have an identity of their own as a person in the world. They do not live in other people's eyes or on other people's terms. They know where other people end and they begin. They are able to cooperate with their fellow human beings without fearing that their selfhood will be compromised or engulfed by others. Nor do they seek to enhance their selfhood by engulfing others. They know that their identity as worthwhile human beings cannot be enhanced nor diminished. They do not play childhood roles in their adult relationships. They

are flexible in their relationships with their spouses, children, bosses, friends and subordinates. They play appropriate adult roles as the changing reality of the situation demands, but they know all the while who and what they really are -- worthwhile human beings in their own right.

4. **Maturity**: Self-respecting people have the feeling that they are at an appropriate stage of development for their age. They will not feel older than their years, nor will they feel childish or faintly ridiculous. They will not be vulnerable to postponing their life until some day in the future when they are grown-up enough to handle it. They will be living their lives in the present and deriving appropriate gratification from it. Under extreme stress, they may find themselves reverting to childhood roles, attitudes and behaviors, but they will have the resilience to recuperate quickly from these temporary regressions.

5. **Belonging**: Self-respecting people do not question their "belongingness." Wherever they go, that's where they belong. They feel themselves to be a member in good standing of the human race. They have a sense of "embeddedness." They belong to themselves, to their family and to their community. They are secure in their belonging. It is not conditional and no one can take this belonging away from them.

6. **Security**: Self-respecting individuals feel secure within themselves. They feel secure in their ability to cope with the ups and downs of life. They do not live in fear of disasters. They do not prophesize disasters in the first place. They know that they can tolerate more distress and pain than they could as a child. They are not afraid of pain, they can take it as it comes. They do not live in the future, which is a setup for insecurity. They live in the present.

7. **Trust**: Self-respecting individuals can trust others because they trust themselves. They trust their own ability to

discriminate between people who are worthy of their trust and those who are not. Even if their judgment isn't perfect, they can trust their competence to deal with a mistaken judgment if and when it happens. It will not shake their trust in their judgment -- it will only prove that their judgment isn't perfect. It is still good enough.

8. **Equality:** Self-respecting individuals do not feel inferior to others, nor do they feel the need to overcompensate by imagining themselves to be superior. They are not consciously aware that they feel like an equal human being, but they do and they behave accordingly. They can respect themselves in the presence of the governor, as well as in the presence of children.

9. **Relief from Guilt:** Self-respecting individuals are less prone to feeling guilty than individuals with self-contempt. If they make a mistake, they don't feel guilty of failing to live up to expectations. They perceive it in the context of their human imperfection and they can learn from it.

If they should behave inappropriately, as imperfect people do, they don't wallow in useless, phony guilt feelings. They are able to take appropriate remedial action and to feel active remorse to an appropriate degree. They "know" consciously or not, that imperfection is not a crime.

10. **Liberation:** Individuals who come to respect themselves feel liberated, not from the demands and expectations of others, but from their vulnerability to them. They feel liberated from the carryover attitudes and mispreceptions that have been interfering with their happiness and success since childhood. They are no longer a victim, they can deal effectively with those who seek to victimize them. They are no longer a rebel, mindlessly reacting when they don't get their way. They can solve problems constructively and choose to make other arrangements. They feel liberated from their childhood roles, fears and doubts. They will have the feeling that they have liberated themselves, which is the

only way that it can be done. They cannot begin to liberate anyone until they have liberated themselves. Once they have done so, they will be able to set an example of liberation for other people to follow if they choose.

11. Independence: Having liberated themselves, self-respecting individuals have the feeling that they are independent entities in their own right. They are not dependent on others to validate their existence as a person in the world. They can and do validate their own worth in spite of their faults and imperfections. They are now free to enter and maintain interdependent relationships with other independent human beings as equals.

12. Accomplishment: When self-respecting individuals complete a task, they experience a feeling of accomplishment. They do not undo or minimize their achievement. They can accept appropriate commendation for their accomplishment. They know what they did and they know that it was good enough. They know that they can build on it in the future and they know that they did it.

13. Success: These individuals are free to experience themselves as having succeeded. They have earned the right to feel successful -- they deserve it. Since their effectiveness in the world is no longer hampered by self-doubt, they are more likely to succeed at solving problems than they were before they acquired their self-respect. They are not driven to succeed, they are free to succeed.

14. Courage to Succeed: Self-respecting people are not afraid that their success in the present will lead to higher expectations which they will fail to achieve. They take success, like failure, as it comes. They feel that they deserve to succeed, no more and no less than anyone else. They do not fear that their happiness will end in disaster. They do not abort their happiness in order to get it over with. They can tolerate success.

15. **Confidence**: Having succeeded once, they have every right to conclude that they can do it again. They are also confident that their worth as a person is not threatened by the ups and downs of life. They feel adequately prepared to take them as they come.

16. **Courage:** Self-respecting people are willing to take appropriate risks. They can draw confidence from their successes. They become willing to take the greater risks that life requires them to take. They can discriminate between those risks that need to be taken and those that do not. They are no longer discouraged. In having the courage to make success happen, they have encouraged themselves. They do not wait for the courage to come. They go ahead and do it anyway. The courage comes afterward.

17. **Appropriate Responsibility:** They are able to assume as much responsibility as the situation demands, not too much and not too little. They are able to assess the situation objectively and to respond appropriately to it. They know that there are no rights without responsibility, and they are willing to pay that price.

18. **Appropriate Anger:** When we respect ourselves, we are enabled to respond appropriately to anger-provoking situations. We do not get angrier than we need to be, nor do we deny or suppress our anger. We feel free to express our legitimate anger in a mature, responsible way. We have the responsibility and the right to do so.

20. **Trusting Our Judgment:** Self-respecting people learned in childhood or through counseling that their judgment can be trusted. It isn't perfect, but it doesn't have to be. It is good enough. They do not prevent mistakes by refusing to decide. They trust their competence to take the appropriate corrective action if their judgment turns out to be mistaken.

21. **Power of Choice:** Because self-respecting individuals respect their judgment, they are free to make choices. They know that they can live with the consequences of their decisions. If they

are mistaken, they know that they can learn from their mistakes and correct them. They appreciate their freedom to make choices and they are prepared to assume the responsibilities that go with that freedom.

22. **Intellectual Self-Respect:** This feeling can be expressed as, "As smart as I am right now, that is smart enough. If I am smarter still tomorrow, that is all right too. In the meantime, I am smart enough."

23. **Self-Acceptance:** Self-respecting people accept themselves as they are right now. They do not qualify their self-acceptance in terms of such external considerations as appearance, popularity, success, intelligence, sexual prowess or athletic achievement. They feel "good enough." They do not require themselves to feel any better than that.

24. **Counting Their Blessings:** Self-respecting individuals recognize their blessings and appreciate them appropriately. They are content. It is enough. If more comes tomorrow, that will be enough too.

25. **Securing Cooperation:** People who respect themselves are free to solve problems by securing the cooperation of their fellow human beings. They do not submit, nor do they require others to submit to them. Because they respect themselves, other people are more likely to respect them and to cooperate with them in an atmosphere of mutual respect.

26. **Acceptance of Unpleasant Reality:** Self-respecting people are not vulnerable to taking a mishap as a personal affront. They are not devastated when they do not get their own way. It is not the end of the world. It is only a disaster if they don't learn from it. They do not resign themselves to life, they accept it as it comes and do the best they can with it, even under difficult circumstances.

27. **Living in the Present:** People who have self-respect are able to experience themselves as functioning effectively in the real world right now. They do not wallow in the past, nor do they try to prevent the future. They are prepared to take life as it comes and do the best they can with it. They can learn from the past and make effective preparations for the future, but they do it in the present.

28. **Approachable:** Because they accept themselves as worthwhile, they are prepared to accept others as being worthwhile also. Other people sense their openness, trust and appropriate regard for them as equals. Other self-respecting people find these qualities attractive and seek them out.

29. **Unselfish:** People who have an appropriate regard for themselves as worthwhile human beings in spite of their faults and imperfections are free to give of themselves to their fellow human beings. They are not afraid that their gift of self will be rejected as worthless. They are free to receive from others as well. Their ability to accept the offerings of others is not impeded by feelings of unworthiness or guilt. They know that the more they give, the happier they will be, but that's not why they do it. They do it because it is appropriate. They can even give to themselves. They can do what pleases them without overdoing it.

30. **Social Interest:** Self-respecting people are free to have an appropriate regard for the welfare of their fellow human beings. They are not driven by self-serving, overcompensatory good intentions, nor are they wallowing in miserly self-interest. They understand that the better off the community is, the better off they and their children will be. They can serve the community in a spirit of enlightened self-interest. They do not operate out of mindless idealism, nor do they sink into despair when society does not measure up to their expectations or when society does not express sufficient gratitude for their exertions in its behalf. They do what they feel they have to do. They do not care too much, or too little. They care just enough to do the things that need to be done.

31. Lovability: People who have self-respect feel that they are capable of being loved. They do not compare themselves unfavorably to movie stars or athletes who seem to be more lovable than they are. Nor do they compare themselves favorably to persons who have apparent difficulty in finding a mate. They do not define their worth as a person in terms of being loved by a particular member of the opposite sex. They are, therefore, less vulnerable to being personally devastated by the loss of that love. They are able to relieve their distress somewhat by reminding themselves that they are worthwhile human beings in spite of this loss. They are confident that, having found this love, they are quite capable of finding the next one.

32. In Touch with Reality: People who have a realistic perception of themselves as a person of worth in the world are in a much better position to perceive the world around them objectively and appropriately than those whose perception of the world is clouded by self-doubt and despair. They are also more likely to respond to emotional situations with the appropriate affective reaction. They are more likely to have success in solving their life problems and in relating to their fellow human beings than those whose perception is impaired by feelings of worthlessness. Because they trust their competence to cope with reality, they have fewer crises in their lives.

33. Tolerance of Pain: Self-respecting people do not make the pain of their existence worse than it needs to be. They don't make the mistake of taking their pain as a punishment for their guilt, nor as a reflection on their worth as a person. They do not take their pain as a personal victimization. They do not spend their life trying to prevent pain and they do not blame themselves for failing when they cannot do it. They can learn useful lessons about themselves, others and about life from the unhappy, disappointing events that befall them as they do everyone else.

34. **Positive Compatibility:** If our parents have set an example of self-respect, mutual respect and cooperative problem solving, we will be compatible with self-respecting life partners. We will not be compatible with mischief makers, excitement-seekers or negative role players. We will deserve to be happy and will enjoy making each other happy. We will trust each other positively, not negatively. We will belong to ourselves and each other.

35. **Relief From Fear and Anxiety:** Self-respecting people do not terrify themselves with predictions of failure and disaster in the future. They live in the present. They do not live on the unpredictable terms of other people; they have their own valid terms. They do not set themselves up for scary failure by requiring perfection of themselves. They feel adequately prepared to take life as it comes. They express their anger appropriately in the present so that it does not go out of control and give rise to feelings of anxiety and paranoia.

36. **Not Vulnerable to Temptation:** Self-respecting people do not need exciting mischief to relieve the pain of their existence. They strengthen their self-worth by making appropriate, responsible choices. They can pass up opportunities to engage in self-destructive mischief, not because they are morally superior but because it is inconsistent with the way they feel about themselves. They deserve to be happy in constructive, productive ways. They even deserve to enjoy their happiness.

Self-respecting people are able to resist temptation, not because they are terrified of the consequences, but because self-indulgent, destructive behavior is inconsistent with their self-respect. They can also resist the temptation to stand in moral judgment upon their more vulnerable fellows. They are not moral because of promised rewards here or in the life to come. They are moral because the situation demands it and it is appropriate. They cannot do otherwise. Immorality is inconsistent with their self-respect.

37. **Serenity:** Self-respecting individuals are no longer at war with themselves. They do not hate their human shortcomings or themselves for having them. They do not compare themselves unfavorably to people who are luckier or better than they are. They experience peace of mind, peace of soul and serenity. They do not live in fear that their inadequacies will be revealed, and they do not strive to prove their worth through endless overcompensation. They are not afraid of losing control. They are at peace with themselves and are free to be at peace with their neighbors.

There are, of course, many more facets of self-respect, but these examples will serve to demonstrate the complexity of this very basic human emotion. If our basic attitudes and feelings about ourselves are appropriately positive and realistic, then our thoughts, expectations and behaviors will be positive and effective. The rewards for our effectiveness in the world will be appropriately gratifying and will provide us with a reasonable basis for expecting continued success in the future. We will be free to cooperate appropriately with other self-respecting human beings in the accomplishment of our life tasks -- the tasks of love, work and friendship. This includes the task of building a better, saner world for our children and our children's children.

AFTERWORD

You have come a long way since you first sat down to read this book, and we hope that you have learned some things about anger that you did not know before. We further hope:

1. That you have had a chance to do homework in the real world and that, as a consequence, your anger illiteracy has been replaced by anger literacy.

2. That your angerphobia has been replaced by the courage to take appropriate risks.

3. That you now have choices that you did not have before.

4. That you can now solve problems that "nice" people weren't even supposed to have.

We also hope that you can apply these techniques in your own life as you weather the ups and downs at home and at work. Your success with these new choices will serve as a model for other people to follow, should they choose to. By your example, you will be spreading the word that anger is a legitimate part of the human condition and that it can be managed if you know how.

This book wasn't just about anger, was it? It is a handbook of psychotherapy that counselors, teachers and other helpers can use to understand their clients' anger problems in a new light. Anger is not a mysterious instinct or an irresistible natural force. It is an emotional response to a grievance. Human beings can learn to perceive their grievances in less painful ways, thereby relieving the consequent emotional pain. The reduced pain is more manageable -- it helps even more when we have tools to manage it with. The emotional pain goes away sooner when you know what is going on.

Anger therapy techniques are not restricted to psychological practitioners. They are useful to nonprofessionals, such as parents, siblings, neighbors, co-workers and everyone else who deals with imperfect human beings on a daily basis.

We understand our fellow human beings as people who are trying to relieve their painful feelings of inferiority and inadequacy through overcompensatory striving for superiority. If not positive superiority, then negative superiority will do. This understanding of human nature is based on the psychology of Alfred Adler and Rudolph Dreikurs. We have included some of their books as references for additional reading. We find this school of psychology to be very practical and immediate. Once we identify negative behavior as overcompensatory mischief, we are enabled to cope with it more successfully. We can stop taking the misbehavior personally and begin to disengage from it. The results are often gratifying to us and to the individual who was misbehaving. These negative behaviors can now be replaced with more constructive ones -- to the benefit of all.

We encourage you to use this book as a resource for yourself and to share it with others. When you see someone struggling with an anger situation that you have read about, show them the page and let them learn for themselves about the new choices they have available to them. They will be relieved, and so will you. That is not just a good intention -- it is a real intention.

This book is not a substitute for competent counseling. We are too close to the problems and cannot see ourselves as others see us. We may have to pay someone to give us the feedback about our attitudes and behaviors that we cannot give ourselves. In the meantime, there are the emotional cuts and bruises of everyday life that do not require the services of a professionally trained practitioner. We can learn to take the sting out of an anger attack by disengaging from it emotionally and choosing to say, *"I"m sorry you're so angry. "* How many hours of our lives are wasted every year in painful, useless skirmishes over who has the right to be angry at whom?

Trust is an emotion, too, and it sometimes needs first aid. For instance, if we do not know that we are abusing a loved one's trust, we are liable to lose it forever. The emotional cost of this silent, invisible loss is beyond calculation.

Other publications in this series will provide you with helpful suggestions on how to understand and cope with such emotional pathologies as "Negative Excitement," which is a major factor in self-destructive behavior; "Painful Pleasure" which is a commonly overlooked determinant in addictive behavior; the "Abandoned Child Syndrome," which often contributes to the breakup of relationships without either party knowing about it; the "Super Self-Reliant Child," the "Perfect Child," the "Understanding Child" and many more topics relating to mistaken attitudes that we have brought into the present from our childhood past.

These mistaken attitudes contribute to our difficulty in adapting to the everyday tasks of love, work and friendship. They contribute to our negative perception of ourselves and predispose us to behave in counterproductive ways.

"Emotional First Aid" enables us to identify these splinters in our personhood and pluck them out. Each time we succeed, we replace our self-doubt with another dollop of self-respect. We have given ourselves the prerequisite for happiness. Before we can be happy, we must find out who we are. Who are we? We are worthwhile human beings in spite of our faults and imperfections.

P.S.   "Emotional First Aid," can be construed as "What To Do Until The Psychiatrist Comes. . . ." He isn't coming.

REFERENCES

Adler, A. (1968). *The Practice and Theory of Individual Psychology.* New York: Littlefield, Adams & Co.

Adler, A. (1964). *Social Interest: A Challenge to Mankind.* New York: Capricorn Books.

Angier, Natalie (1990). *Chronic Anger May Lead to Early Death.* Chicago: Chicago Tribune, December 20.

Dinkmeyer, D. & McKay, G. (1973). *Raising A Responsible Child.* New York: Simon & Schuster.

Dreikurs, R. Grunwald, B. & Pepper, F. (1971). *Maintaining Sanity in the Classroom.* New York: Harper & Row.

Dreikurs, R. & Grey, L. (1968). *Logical Consequences: A New Approach to Discipline.* New York: Hawthorn Books.

Dreikurs, R. & Soltz, V. (1964), *Children: The Challenge.* New York: Hawthorn Books.

Gilbert, Jerrold I. (1986). *Logical Consequences: A New Classification.* Individual Psychology. 42:2:243-254.

Kübler-Ross, E. (1969). *On Death and Dying.* New York: MacMillan Publishing Co.

Montagu, Ashley (1973). *Man and Aggression.* London: Oxford University Press.

Mosak, Harold H. (1977). *On Purpose.* Chicago: Alfred Adler Institute of Chicago.

Peele, Stanton (1976). *Love and Addiction.* New York: New American Library.

Peele, Stanton (1989). *The Diseasing of America.* New York: New American Library.

Powers, R. & Griffith, J. (1987). *Understanding Life-Style: The Pyscho-Clarity Process.* Chicago: The American Institute of Adlerian Studies, Ltd.

Siegel, Bernie S. (1986). *Love, Medicine and Miracles.* New York: Harper and Row.

Stein, H. (1991). *Adler & Socrates: Similarities and Difference.* Journal of Individual Psychology. 47:2:241-246. University of Texas Press.

Tavris, Carol, (1989). *Anger, The Misunderstood Emotion.* New York: Simon and Schuster.

INDEX